ETHICAL ISSUES IN COUNSELING

ETHICAL
ISSUES
IN
COUNSELING

RONALD H. STEIN

PROMETHEUS BOOKS
Buffalo, New York

Published 1990 by Prometheus Books
700 East Amherst Street, Buffalo, New York 14215

Library of Congress Cataloging-in-Publication Data

Stein, Ronald H.
    Ethical issues in counseling / by Ronald H. Stein
        p.   cm.
    Includes bibliographical references.
    ISBN 0-87975-557-1
    1. Counseling—Moral and ethical aspects. 2. Counselors—Professional
ethics. I. Title.
BF637.C6S755   1990
174'.915—dc20   89-49689
                                                                      CIP

Printed on acid-free paper in the United States of America

Acknowledgments

I would like to pay tribute to a number of special people whose contributions made this book possible. I am indebted to Thomas Webb and Kathryn A. Myers, who have provided invaluable assistance in editing the manuscript. My special thanks goes to Susan-Marie Fonzi, who worked many long hours in preparing and typing the manuscript. Finally, I want to thank Andrea, Matthew, Ethan, and Erica, whose patience, understanding, and sacrifice made this book possible.

This book is dedicated to the memory of Theodore Buyer.

Contents

8   Contents

1

Introduction

Historically, those who have dedicated their lives to helping others have struggled with ethical issues. During the Middle Ages physicians frequently confronted the question of "the right thing to do" with the knowledge that a fellow villager had the plague. It is reported that during this time the problem of how to deal with the spread of highly contagious diseases gave rise to the Anglo-Saxon notion of privilege and confidentiality; the same concepts of confidentiality we hold so dearly today. (It is interesting to note the parallel dilemma faced by today's health professional regarding information about Acquired Immune Deficiency Syndrome [AIDS]).

Today's counselor throughout the helping professions faces many new ethical challenges while continuing to struggle with traditional moral concerns. Vexing questions arise anew each day: Should I always tell the truth, even if my client will be hurt? How far should I go in protecting my client's rights? How should decisions be made when there is a conflict between ethical values, such as my duty to my client versus my obligation to an agency or employer? What should I do when the wishes of my client, a minor, are in conflict with those of the parents?

Some ethical issues have emerged in the very recent past. With the advent of the microprocessor, health care providers are able to find technological solutions to previously unsolved medical problems. The advance in technology has been so rapid that today we are able to keep individuals "alive" who, just a few short years ago, would have died. These advances are not without their consequences; they raise difficult ethical issues for physicians, counselors, and families. For example, today some intensive care nurseries are able to save over 90 percent of all their premature babies. In the past, many of these babies would have died shortly after birth. Unfortunately, some of these newborns face a sharply reduced life expectancy, severe physical/mental handicaps, or a combination of factors. Ethically we find ourselves suddenly facing the question of when to choose between life and death. Is it possible to determine the potential quality of an individual life? Should factors pertaining to the quality of potential life affect the choices we make?

In much the same way, other advances in technology have given rise to similar dilemmas. Today, it is possible to maintain a person's biological functions even though the brain has died. Nearly everyone has heard or read of cases where life support maintained a patient whose brain wave scan (EEG) demonstrated no discernible activity. In some cases, this is done not because it is believed that the person will recover, but because technology has made possible organ transplantation. The individual's life becomes valuable in death because it is possible for that person to give life to others. As organ transplants become more commonplace a greater demand for organs will develop. However, the supply will remain limited, given the present state of our knowledge and current methods of preserving organs. In the future, we may find a delicate balance developing between a person's right to die in peace and the need to keep a patient alive by artificial means so that organs can be "harvested." What rights do the living have versus the rights of a person in death?

Finally, contemporary society is struggling with a very basic ethical question—can suicide be rational? Again, as a result of medical advances and a broader social awareness of individual rights, we are seriously debating the question of euthanasia in both the courtroom and in the classroom. This is just one of society's many struggles with value-laden questions. The struggle is not new. Social, economic, cultural, and religious conditions have historically played a role in determining what is normal and what is abnormal. Consider the following three examples.

"Benjamin Rush (1805), the father of American psychiatry, discovered a new form of psychosis which he called Revolutiona. The symptom of Revolutiona was resistance to the American Revolution among colonists" (Weisskopf-Jackson, 1980, p. 459). "Samuel Cartwright, a psychiatrist from New Orleans, discovered, around 1850, a new form of psychosis which he called Drapetomania. Medical records indicate that not a single white patient has ever suffered from this kind of psychosis. Instead, the 'disease' was limited to black slaves. Drapetomania means 'run-away-from-home mania,' and the symptom of the disease was the slaves' running away from their masters" (Weisskopf-Jackson, 1980, p. 459).

Until 1974, the American Psychiatric Association classified homosexuality as a disease requiring treatment. That year the APA voted on the status of homosexuality. "The vote showed that homosexuality is not a disease, which was contrary to the opinion held in the past" (Weisskopf-Jackson, 1980, p. 459-60).

In this book I intend to raise the most common ethical issues faced by counselors in the helping professions. It is hoped that a systematic consideration of these issues will raise the consciousness of counselors with respect to the ethical dimensions of their professional behavior. I seek to provide counselors with an opportunity to explore their own ethical values in the context of problematic situations and, in doing so, it is hoped that these professionals will be better prepared to serve their clients. Counselors will, I believe, derive some personal benefit from this exercise. First, professionals will, perhaps for the first time, have an opportunity to take a close look at their own values. Second, the counselor will have an opportunity to consider whether these values are in fact the ones they prefer. This exercise may encourage counselors to ask: "Does this truly reflect who I am and what I want to be?" In an effort to prepare professionals to answer this question, the present volume begins with a detailed discussion of a number of fundamental concerns, including the nature of ethics and why counselors should be concerned with it. But, before considering the nature of ethics, let us first discuss what it means to say that counseling is a profession.

THE NATURE OF THE PROFESSION

Society bestows upon individuals engaged in certain occupations the status of "professional." Counselors* enjoy the privileges and responsibilities of membership in a profession. But what does it mean to say that someone is a professional? Here are some of the necessary elements of a profession:

*For the purpose of this book I have chosen to use the terms "counselor," "psychotherapist," and "therapist" interchangeably. I conceive of a counselor as a professional who has demonstrated competence by mastering a unique curriculum and having been certified as such by receiving a degree or certificate from an accredited counseling program.

Education

A profession has a unique subject matter, most often devoted to mental rather than manual skills. Members of a profession receive training in a specialized subject matter usually at the postbaccalaureate level. The conferring of a degree (e.g., M.D., D.D.S., J.D., B.S., Ph.D., M.S.W., and so forth) symbolizes satisfactory completion of formalized training. The course of study is reviewed regularly by an accrediting agency to ensure that it meets the minimum standards of the profession. In addition, the course of study and the degrees conferred are registered and approved by an appropriate state agency, again to ensure that the curriculum meets certain standards.

It is important to note that the review and quality control of academic standards by accrediting bodies is designed only to certify that the academic program provides appropriate professional training by a particular institution, which meets minimum standards. Academic institutions do not certify that a person is competent to practice as a professional. (For example, law schools do not pass judgment on whether their graduates meet the appropriate ethical standards to practice law. That task belongs to the local Bar Association's Ethics Review Committee.)

Licensure

Most professions require that individuals be licensed before they can practice, especially where private patients and third party payments are involved. Licensing is provided by a state agency, usually a branch of the state department of education, which has minimum educational requirements, but also includes moral character and the like.

Freedom and Autonomy

Professionals exercise a greater degree of control over their jobs than do nonprofessionals. They may set fees for their services and establish work hours. Professionals have a greater degree of control over the services they provide. They exercise a wide-range discretion in deciding on the best way(s) to achieve the end(s) desired by their clients. Professionals have a substantial degree of freedom in representing the interests of their clients: some professionals may speak for and/or enter into obligations on behalf of their clients. Because of the esoteric nature of professional skills, their actions are generally above reproach vis-à-vis the general public, except by a colleague possessing similar expertise who is thought competent to judge.

Calling

Moore (1970) argues that "calling" is one of the ways to characterize individual commitment to a profession. "Commitment to a calling involves acceptance of the appropriate norms and standards, and identification with professional peers and the profession as a collectivity" (p. 8).

Professional Association

Important to the profession is the existence of a professional association whose members have adopted a set of performance standards in the form of an ethical code. This set of standards establishes guidelines for the appropriate behavior of members. (Chapter 5 is devoted to a more detailed discussion of professional codes of ethics.) In addition to these professional standards, the association has an adjudication procedure through which each member can be charged with violating its standards. This procedure outlines the manner in which the charges against a member are resolved, the rights of the accused, and sanctions (including expulsion from the profession) that may be assessed against members who are found guilty of violating the standards.

It is important to note that interests of the organization focus primarily on professional status rather than on terms and conditions of employment. These include: "(a) recognition of common occupational interests, with some priority over all other simultaneously competing interests; (b) some mechanism of control to maintain standards of performance; and (c) control of access to the occupation, so that qualifications for inclusion are essentially under the control and jurisdiction of current practitioners" (Moore, 1970, p. 10).

Professional Service

Members of a profession are expected to place the interests of their clients and society above self-interest. Members agree to provide their clients with a minimum level of service. This level of professional competence is ensured by adherence to the ethical codes of the organization. Also, members of some professions are required to maintain their skills and to demonstrate that these skills have been maintained by successfully passing continuing education courses.

Professional Duty

A duty is owed by professionals to their clients. That duty may be established in a number of different ways. For example, in private practice a duty is established because clients pay professionals a fee for services rendered. Upon receipt and acceptance of the fee, it is the professional's obligation (duty) to provide the service. Most professionals who are employed in public service positions have a similar duty: it may be set forth in a contract between the employee and the employer, or in a collective bargaining agreement between the employer and the employee union, or in the form of a job description outlining the duties and responsibilities of the employee.

The notion of duty is especially important because it distinguishes a professional from those who act as volunteers or good Samaritans, and because it forms one of the necessary conditions in the legal concept of malpractice. It is through the notion of duty that we hold professionals accountable not only for providing a service but for providing it at a level of competency that satisfies a set of standards, be it an organization's code of professional ethics or standards measured against the performance levels of other professionals in the community where the particular professional in question practices. Moore (1970) calls these standards "general performance norms," which, he says, "refer primarily to the professional's obligations to clients, but secondarily to peers, since incompetent or slovenly performance, or failure to protect a client's interests, necessarily reflects discredit on the professional collectivity. Indeed, the general functions of performance norms are, ideally, both to protect the ignorant client and the legitimate practitioner against the charlatan or the improper practitioner" (p. 14).

We will see in future chapters that while the concept of duty is central for defining a professional, it becomes very ambiguous and confusing when we ask the question, "Who is our client?" In other words, unto whom is the duty owed? Are the clients those who pay for the services? That seems reasonable for, after all, in private practice clients come to professionals and pay a fee for which these professionals provide services directly to the clients in the form of counseling.

Unfortunately, the relationship is not always so clear. Take, for example, school counselors: the question of who the client is, i.e., to whom the counselors' primary duty is owed, becomes slightly more confusing. If we posit that the client is the person who pays for the service, it would appear that we should conclude that the client is the board of education whose agent is the school principal. But the direct beneficiary of services is the person who is directly advised and counseled. If we were to apply the private practice model, there would be no question that the pupil would be the client. The situation becomes further complicated if it turns out that the student is a minor, in which case the counselor may have a duty and obligation to the parents. Finally, the same situation can be complicated still further if there has been judicial intervention. For example, perhaps a judge has granted a motion to declare the counselor's client a "Person In Need of Supervision" (PINS).

The question of who the client is should not be viewed as purely academic: the answer is important in determining from whom a counselor obtains informed consent, who is entitled to confidential information, who participates in planning the course of treatment, and many other significant elements of the counselor-client relationship. This question will be explored further in chapter 3. Now let us turn our attention to ethics and its application to the counselor.

REFERENCES

Moore, W. E. 1970. *The Professions: Roles and Rules,* New York: Russell Sage Foundation.

Weisskopf-Jackson, E. 1980. "Value: The Enfant Terrible of Psychotherapy," *Psychotherapy: Theory Research and Practice* **17** (4), 459.

2

Ethics and the Counselor

Philosophers in Western society have been concerned with the ethics of human conduct for over two thousand years (e.g., Socrates, 470–399 B.C.) and in Eastern societies even longer (e.g., Confucius, 555–479 B.C.). However, the interest in applied ethics is very recent, dating back to the mid-1970s with the real momentum building in the 1980s. There is evidence to conclude that there has been a similar growing interest in ethics by members of the counseling profession. This interest manifests itself in the form of professional organizations choosing ethics as the theme for their national, state, or local meetings. Publishers are anxious for books on the topic of ethical issues in counseling, more universities are offering courses on the theme, and more students are registering for these courses. Professional journals are eager to publish articles on the theme of ethics because they know the appeal that these articles have to the journal's readership.

Why this sudden rush of interest in the ethical concerns of counselors? To a large extent, what we take to be a growing interest in ethics among counselors is in fact a confusion between ethical and legal issues. Those who offer this argument explain that what we are seeing is really an interest in such legal issues as liability. Counselors are confused about the difference between legal and ethical issues, especially at the point where legal issues end and ethical issues begin.

Certainly there is reason to believe that this argument has merit. Recent

17

events in the counseling profession such the Tarasoff decision in California*
and the crisis of malpractice throughout the country tend to focus our
attention on issues that straddle the legal-ethical line of demarcation. Additional legal/quasi-ethical issues of current concern to counselors include:
When does good practice become malpractice? What are the elements of
informed consent? Has informed consent become, for the client, what the
Miranda warnings are for the defendant?† Are there any limits to the
client's right to know? Must counselors inform clients about their professional training? Must counselors inform clients about any malpractice
suits they may have lost? These are just some of the legal issues of substantial
concern to the counseling profession. However, are these the issues that
really concern the counselor rather than the desire to do the right thing
in a situation regardless of whether or not it is legally mandated?

Another hypothesis has been offered to explain the burgeoning interest
in ethical issues for counselors: some believe it is driven by the demands
of the professional organizations and the accrediting bodies (agencies). On
this view, the graduate programs in counseling are finally listening to the
clarion call of the professional organizations, i.e., that students in these
programs need to be schooled in the ethical issues that impact their
profession. Accrediting bodies are beginning to enforce the views of professional organizations by requiring curricular change to ensure that survey
courses do not ignore ethical issues. It would not be surprising to see,
in the very near future, accrediting bodies requiring a full-semester course
on ethical issues.

A third theory is that counselors' interest in ethics is one example
of the fall-out from the high technology revolution in which our society
currently finds itself. As technology becomes more and more a part of
our daily experience, we become more dependent upon it to solve our
problems and to improve the quality of our lives. However, we are dis-
covering that "progress" comes with certain costs. The price of technology
includes both environmental and human consequences. The former include
toxic wastes, nuclear hazards, and acid rain, to name just a few. The

---

*In *Tarasoff* the California Supreme Court ruled that if a psychologist has determined
that his client is a danger to others, he has a duty to warn the intended victim. In *Tarasoff*
the intended victim was out of the country, but the court found the psychologist negligent
because he failed to notify the victim's parents of his client's expressed intent to kill their
daughter.

†Miranda warnings are a statement of rights provided to an arrested person, which
he must understand and waive before a court of law will allow any statements made
by him to be admissible as evidence.

latter include the price of knowledge, quality versus quantity of life, and a concern about the impact of high technology on the human condition. Concern over the use of human subjects in research has raised an important question: What price is society prepared to pay in the pursuit of knowledge? This question has been clearly answered: no individual should risk physical or psychological harm without first giving informed consent. In the course of asserting the priority of human rights over scientific rights, we have said that there may be some knowledge that we just can't afford because it exacts too great a toll in human suffering.

Another human consequence of the technological revolution is that it makes very real the debate between the mere existence (quantity) of life and the quality of that life. Technological advances have given us the means to save, preserve, and prolong life, but not without a price. Respirators and renal dialysis have prompted debate and efforts to refine the definition of death. "Technologies, such as mechanical ventilation and renal dialysis, provide powerful tools that permit prolonged survival of patients who previously would have succumbed to their illnesses before the quality of their lives would have become an issue" (Spritz, 1988, p. 24).

The growing success of organ transplants is another arena of ethical concern, the dynamics of which are almost beyond comprehension. Experimentation in this delicate frontier of medicine contraposes two fundamental human principles: the right to live versus the right to die with dignity. Further complicating matters are the religious principles of reincarnation and salvation, since each has served to stretch the limits of our conceptions of life and death. In addition, society must address a number of related ethical questions: How do we choose wisely between individuals making competing claims for the right to life? Who should receive transplants, and if need be, to how many such transplants is a person entitled? Is it right for one person to undergo three transplants while three other people die for lack of such surgery? Is it morally justified to allow patients to die because they cannot afford the high cost of an organ transplant?

Breakthroughs in technology have made it possible to save very small, premature babies with birth defects who, a few short years ago, would not have survived. In addition, the advances of technology and modern medicine have made it possible to save premature babies with low birth weight, many of whom are severely handicapped or have substantially reduced life expectancies. Our sophisticated medical achievements have forced us to focus attention on the essential tension between the preservation or maintenance of life and quality of that life. In the words of Sidney Hook:

We may define the good differently, but no matter what our conception of the good life is, it presupposes a physical basis—a certain indispensable minimum of physical and social well-being—necessary for even a limited realization of that good life. Where that minimum is failing, together with all rational probability of attaining it, to avoid a life that at its best can be only vegetative and at its worst run the entire gamut of degradation and obloquy, what high-minded person would refuse the call of a poet *mourir entre les bras du sommeil* [to die in the arms of sleep]? We must recognize no categorical imperative "to live" but "to live well." (Edwards, 1967, vol. 8, p. 45)

It is a mistake to believe that advanced technology always improves the human condition, for, in fact, most times all it does is give us choices, but never the wisdom to make the best choice. That is a question technology cannot solve. Instead, we must look within ourselves for the answer.

Bioethics and counseling ethics are two manifestations of a growing concern for the human condition. We must look beyond our technology and toward the human being. We may indeed be returning to the Socratic notion of the whole man in whom physical, intellectual, and moral development were equally valued. Perhaps these growing concerns about the ethical behavior of counselors are nothing more than contemporary manifestations captured in the words of Sam Johnson, who wrote:

The truth is that knowledge of external nature, and the sciences which that knowledge requires or includes are not the great or the frequent business of the human mind. Whether we provide for action or conversation, whether we wish to be useful or pleasing, the first requisite is the religious and moral knowledge of right and wrong, the next is an aquaintance with the history of mankind, and with those examples which may be said to embody truth, and prove by events the reasonableness of opinions. Prudence and Justice are virtues in excellence of all times and of all places; we are perpetually moralists, but we are geometricians only by chance. (quoted in Krutch, 1959, p. 200)

Whatever the reason, the professional literature demonstrates a rapidly growing interest among counselors in the ethical issues that affect their practice. But why should counselors be interested in ethics?

There are numerous reasons for counselors to have a special obligation to be ethical—an obligation that transcends their role as private citizens. The first obligation stems from the nature of the profession itself.

Society has long recognized the existence of the "helping professions," a special class of individuals whose duties and responsibilities provide a valuable function to society and, as such, they enjoy certain rights and privileges. The special obligations of these professions can be found enunciated in the preambles of the codes of ethics of the professional counselors organizations. For example, the preamble of the Ethical Principles of Psychology states: "Psychologists respect the dignity and worth of the individual, and strive for the preservation and protection of fundamental human rights. They are committed to increasing knowledge of human behavior and of peoples' understanding of themselves and others and to the utilization of such knowledge for the promotion of human welfare. While pursuing these objectives, [psychologists] make every effort to protect the welfare of those who seek their services and of the research participants that may be the object of study. They use their skills only for purposes consistent with these values and do not normally permit their misuse by others" (APA, 1981, p. 633). The ethical principles of the American Personnel Guidance Association states: "The American Personnel Guidance Association is an educational, scientific, and professional organization whose members are dedicated to the enhancement of the worth, dignity, potential, and uniqueness of each individual and thus to the service of society" (Callis, 1982, p. 9).

Counselors, therefore, should be ethical because society views the members of the "helping professions," as *noblesse oblige:* because of the rights and privileges these professional possess, they incur a special obligation to society. A large part of that obligation is the public's expectation that counselors will act ethically in their professional performance and, as we will see later, at times even in their personal lives. In a very real sense, society has vested counselors with a special trust to rank service to clients above self-interest. This service is defined as the duty to promote the client's goals, including protecting the client's rights, maximizing the client's benefits, and minimizing potential harm. We find, therefore, that the counselor's obligation to be ethical is embodied in the very nature of the profession. It is an essential element for a vocation such as counseling to be classified as a "helping profession": counseling is intrinsically committed to promoting client welfare, and is of special value to our society for precisely that reason. Helping others, it has been argued (Walman, 1982), is the *summum bonum* of all human activity.

The second reason counselors have a special obligation to be ethical arises from the nature of the counselor-client relationship, which is unequal and dominated by the powerful position of the counselor. "Patients enter therapy in need of help and care. By virtue of this fact, they voluntarily submit themselves to an unequal relationship in which their therapists have superior knowledge and power. Transference of feelings, related to the universal childhood experience of dependency on a parent, are inevitably aroused. These feelings further exaggerate the power balance in the therapeutic relationship and render all patients vulnerable to exploitation. The promise to abstain from abusing this position of power for personal gratification is central to the therapeutic contract: violations of this promise destroy the basic trust on which the therapeutic process is founded" (Herman et al., 1987, p. 168).

Counselors must be continually conscious and constantly vigilant of the influence they exert over their clients. They have a moral imperative to evaluate their own behavior to ensure that their actions promote the welfare of clients while minimizing potential harm. Many of the ethical issues that are addressed in subsequent chapters arise because the counselor has failed to recognize the imbalance of power that exists in the counseling relationship.

Also, counselors have a special obligation to act ethically because they are "engaged in intentional or goal-directed activity. The obligation of human service professionals surpasses that of other professionals because those in human services are concerned not only with their own moral actions but with the actions of those served. Whether the counseling goal is health through rehabilitation and 'cure' or the promotion of 'maturity', as demonstrated by enhanced competence, increased autonomy, or improved interpersonal functioning, professional counseling is an educative process committed to valued ends" (Tenneyson & Strom, 1986, p. 298).

Finally, counselors have a special obligation to be ethical because they are engaged in many different forms of moral education with their clients. Part of the counselor's effort is to help clients understand their moral rights and to execute those rights (Leader, 1976; London, 1964; and Tenneyson & Strom, 1986).

Much of the work of counselors is designed to encourage clients to take responsibility for their behavior, to assert their right to be autonomous, and to insist that they be treated fairly and with dignity. The counselor needs to help clients understand the ethical consequences of their decisions and actions, to learn to accept responsibility for those decisions and actions, and to accept the ethical consequences of the choices they make. In spite of what we would like to think, counselors are very much involved in the process of moral education. As teachers, then, counselors have a special obligation to exemplify the highest ethical standards in their professional and personal lives. Let us now move to a discussion of the nature of ethics.

To begin, we need to agree on a working definition of ethics. For the purpose of our topic, ethics for the counseling professions, I have found an excellent "plain language" definition. What is ethics? "First, ethics refers to well-based standards of right and wrong that prescribe what humans ought to do usually in terms of rights, obligations, benefits to society, fairness, or specific virtues.

"Secondly, ethics refers to the study and development of one's ethical standards. . . . It is necessary to constantly examine one's standards to ensure that they are reasonable and well founded. Ethics also means, then, the continuous effort of studying our own moral beliefs and our own moral conduct and striving to ensure that we, and the institutions we help to shape, live up to standards that are reasonable and solidly based" (Andre, 1987, p. 2).

It is argued that all individuals have a personal code of ethics and standards (Lippitt, 1969; Van Hoose, 1980) that they use to guide their actions. People's values represent the totality of their prior experiences derived from environmental influences, education, socialization, and reflection on choices made in other situations. All these factors contribute to a determination of how a person ought to act when confronting a particular situation. Donagan (1962) argues that it is not the actual situation that determines a person's response, but the person's conception of the situation. Therefore, any consideration of ethics must start by recognizing that each individaul comes with an ethical *Weltanschauung,* and counselors are no exception. In the words of Van Hoose and Kottler (1987), "All people have beliefs about how things ought to be or how they would like them to be. We are *for* some things and *against* others; we hold some things to be *good* and others *bad,* some *true* and some *false.* This polarity, however, is not reducible to that between *yes* and *no* in the logical sense, because a thing or action can be partially good and partially bad or at one time right and at another time wrong. And one can equivocate on 'yes' or respond 'no' with finality. The disposition to favor some things and to disfavor others leads, however, to choices and decisions or, to put it more directly, significantly influences the behavior of both client and therapist" (p. 97).

Therefore, in order to become effective, it is fundamentally important that the counselor develop a model of ethical behavior. The first step in such a model is to develop the sensitivity to be able to recognize an ethical problem. Counselors must become sensitive and attentive to the ethical dimensions of counseling, including—but not limited to—the decisions made and actions taken. This ethical sensitivity is important because "ethical issues are not always conspicuous, though they are always present" (Saad, 1988, p. 55). Rest (1984) provides us with a four-step model of ethical behavior, one that is worthy of careful consideration (reported in Biggs & Blocker, 1987). In the initial phase he argues that we must recognize that what we do and what we say in the course of our professional conduct impacts on the lives of others. Counselors are not value-neutral people; they believe some actions to be good and other actions bad. These values are displayed in the choices that they make, the questions they ask, and the advice they offer. This first phase is called "Ethical Sensitivity" (Biggs & Blocker, 1987). "Ethical Sensitivity is essentially a form of empathy" (p. 108). When counselors are ethically sensitive they can see a complex situation from the perspective of their clients, they can feel the consequences of their actions on those who seek their services, and they can feel how their clients are interpreting remarks and projected values (Biggs & Blocker, 1987). Once conscious of the ethical component of their behavior, counselors can then ensure that they are transmitting the appropriate values to their clients. "Component I involves person perception, role taking, imagining consequences of action and how the parties would be affected, as well as constructing mental scenarios of probable causal chains of events set in motion by one's own action" (Rest, 1987, p. 19).

In the words of Biggs and Blocker (1987), "each new client, each new problem or tangled set of relationships that we encounter in clinical practice should move us toward greater and greater capacities for empathetic understanding. As we travel this thorny path of professional development, we become more and more sensitive to ethical issues and concerns" (p. 108).

This increased ethical sensitivity provides the counselor with a sense of satisfaction. At times, however, it is disturbing and puzzling. Again, the words of Biggs and Blocker (1987):

> In one sense, our increased sensitivity deepens our sense of ethical responsibility and sharpens our awareness of the complexity of those ethical situations with which we must deal.
> We realize all too well that clients come to us and to our colleagues precisely because they have confidence in our willingness to struggle responsibly with all of the complexities and ambiguities involved in the real-life situations of which they are a part. (p. 108)

Therefore, counselors' ethical sensitivity is raised by improving their ethical consciousness of the ethical issues that are always inherent in counseling situations. This is accomplished by being trained to ask ethically relevant questions.

Rest (1984) argues that counselors need to make an extraordinary effort to become sensitive to the moral issues in their profession because traditional education programs have neglected this area of counselor education. This training is necessary because, in the words of Rest (1984), "Typical professional education is so focused on the technical aspects of the job that students in graduate programs in most professions are 'professionally socialized' not to look for moral problems or to recognize moral issues in their work" (p. 21).

Therefore, counselors should study ethics so they will be able to understand why individuals (clients and colleagues) act unethically. Also, they will be able to differentiate between ethical and unethical behavior. Training in ethics will help counselors understand what issues are important in resolving ethical dilemmas and enable them to "sort through the complex considerations in making a decision about the ethical course of action in any given situation" (Welfel & Lipsitz, 1983, p. 36).

The second step of Rest's model involves identifying some principle or set of principles that can be used to define obligations and within which individuals can frame their choices (Biggs & Blocker, 1987). These are called "First Order" principles and represent abstract ethical theories against which our ethical action is ultimately justified. As we have already discussed, every counselor has a basic system of ethics to which he subscribes and against which he determines his action. For some this system of ethics is based on religious beliefs. This may be the belief that God gave man commandments, or ethical principles, that govern human conduct. This theory of ethics is the Rule of Authority because God is believed to be the authority from whom we have received our commandments.

The Golden Rule is an excellent example of a moral precept based on the authority of religion. The generally accepted version of the Golden Rule, "Do unto others as you would have others do unto you," can be traced in Western civilization to the Sermon on the Mount (Edwards, 1967, vol. 3). This is viewed by many as a fundamental ethical truth because it is so universally accepted throughout the world. (It has been argued that Confucius had formulated a version of the Golden Rule five hundred years before Christ: "What I do not want others to do to me, I do not want to do to them" (Chang, 1963, p. 28).

Others believe in the natural law theory of ethics; that is, human beings have certain ethical principles that are part of our definition of being human. We have certain inalienable rights, such as the right to life, liberty, and the pursuit of happiness. These rights and others stemming from our nature form part of the fundamental basis upon which we determine our actions.

The other determinants of our action are concomitant obligations that arise parallel with our rights. We call these obligations responsibilities and include among them truth-telling, promise-keeping (fidelity), not doing harm (nonmaleficence), doing good (beneficence), and respecting the rights of our fellow man.

Still others believe that what ought to be done is measured by how many people would be helped and harmed. This theory of the greatest good for the greatest number is known as *utilitarianism*. The reader should be familiar with the difference between "act" utilitarianism and "rule" utilitarianism. By "act" utilitarianism we mean that an act is good if it produces good consequences and bad if it produces bad consequences. Rule utilitarians do not judge an act to be good or bad but rather they judge the rightness or wrongness of the general rule upon which the action was based. That is, a rule is good if adopting it produces better consequences than would be produced if an alternative rule was adopted (Edwards, *Encyclopedia of Philosophy,* 1967, vol. 8).

There are those who believe that men and women are not born with ethical principles, but discover the fundamental values about themselves only by living their lives. This theory of existence prior to essence is what we term *existentialism*. Those who ascribe to these basic ethical tenets discover the true meaning of their existence through the process of making critical choices. In a sense, we become aware of our ethical principles by the choices we make in the lives we live.

Finally, there are those who believe that their ethical choices are determined by the facts of the situation they confront. The fundamental ethical principles we apply in particular situations are determined by the facts of those situations. This allows us the freedom to maximize our ethical conduct while recognizing the need to act differently in different situations.

It is also within the second step that counselors establish a set of "Second Order" principles (Biggs & Blocker, 1987) designed to guide specific behaviors, principles that may come about because these helping professionals believe that this is the way they want to be treated as individuals and as professionals, or principles that may result because they feel it is the right thing to do. Examples of such principles include fidelity.

Fidelity (Kitchener, 1984) is the ethical principle of keeping one's promise. It is basic to the counselor-client relationship. Fidelity is a principle of trust that develops between the counselor and the client in return for the client's willingness to tell the counselor his innermost secrets. In return, clients should expect counselors to be honest, truthful, forthright, and faithful in their dealings with those who seek assistance. Many scholars believe that trust is the cornerstone of the counselor-client relationship. Kitchener (1984) argues that confidentiality is a special form of trust contained in the principle of fidelity. Confidentiality is based upon the counselor's promise not to reveal to anyone communications made by the client in the counseling relationship. It is this promise to honor confidential communications that engenders the client's trust and fosters the free and forthright disclosure of aspects of the client's life that, under any other circumstances, he might refuse to reveal.

Ethical counseling involves respect for the confidential nature of the counseling relationship and only breaches confidentiality under specific, well-circumscribed circumstances, such as protecting life or under lawful court order. The counselor respects a client's freedom of choice, recognizing that adults have a right to determine their own fate, that they are capable of making rational choices, and that he, the counselor, has an obligation to provide his clients with the appropriate information so that they can make an informed choice. This principle posits nothing more than respect for the dignity of the client.

Keeping one's promise is another example of a Second Order ethical principle. This principle recognizes that fundamental to professional and social relationships is the need to enter into contracts, either formal or informal, and the need to assure that the terms and conditions of these agreements will be fulfilled. As we will see in subsequent chapters, the notion of trust between counselor and client is fundamental to an effective counseling relationship.

Counselors also have an ethical responsibility to protect the rights of those who cannot protect their own. This special obligation might take the form of acting *in loco parentis* for those who are incapable of making their own rational choices. Society and its agent, the court, have recognized two classes of individuals who do not have such capacity: children, and adults who are developmentally disabled.

The principle of autonomy recognizes that people are responsible for their own behavior and that individuals have a right to make their own choices and decisions. This principle forms the basis for a number of other ethical principles in counseling. "For example, the concepts of unconditional worth and tolerance for individual differences both imply a respect for others' rights to make their own decisions. Mutual respect, which many see as basic to the therapeutic bond, implies a relationship between individuals, both of whom are regarded as free agents" (Kitchener, 1984, p. 46).

Those who counsel must recognize that adults have a right to determine their own fate, that they are capable of making rational choices, and that counselors have an obligation to provide them with the appropriate information so that they can make an informed choice. This principle posits nothing more than respect for the dignity of the client. Other ethical principles contained within the concept of autonomy include the right to privacy, the right to informed consent (discussed in chapter 3), and the right to enter into contracts.

The ethical concept of nonmaleficence can be traced to the oath of Hippocrates: "I will apply dietetic measures for the benefit of the sick according to my ability and judgment; I will keep them from harm and injustice" (Etziony, 1973, p. 13). Kitchener (1984) defines this principle as "Above all, do no harm," which "includes both not inflicting intentional harm and [not] engaging in actions which risk harming others" (p. 47). Other ethical principles that arise from the concept of nonmaleficence include nondiscrimination and competence. The counselor is morally obligated not to violate the client's civil rights, including discrimination based on race, color, creed, national origin, age, handicapping condition, sex, sexual preference, and citizenship.

Beneficence (Kitchener, 1984) is the ethical principle by which counselors are obligated to promote the client's good. Counselors have an affirmative moral obligation to help the client, to act so as to benefit the client, to promote client welfare and maximize the client's good. Beneficence is one of the fundamental ethical principles in counseling and is manifested in the notion that counseling is one of the helping professions.

Another ethical principle basic to counseling is that of justice (Kitchener, 1984). Unlike other ethical principles, the definition of justice is broader than benevolence or nonmalevolence. Justice, in one sense, means fair play or fair action. In this sense of the word we are reminded of the Golden Rule: "Do unto others as you would have them do unto you." The counselor should treat the client honestly, trustingly, forthrightly, compassionately, helpfully—the way the counselor would like to be treated. These are the words connoted by the concept of fair play. The notion of justice also implies equality, which is the sense of the word that the philosopher Aristotle employed. He felt that all people should be treated the same unless there was sufficient reason to treat them differently, and only if those differences were relevant to the matter at hand, and in proportion to those differences (Edwards, 1967, vol. 4). For counselors, this means that all clients should be treated the same unless there is something relevant to a client that justifies his counselor treating him differently, for example, when the client is a minor or is developmentally disabled. In other words, unless there is a relevant difference, all clients have the right to equal opportunity for service from the counselor.

Finally, counselors believe a priori in the sanctity of human life, a belief that life is intrinsically valuable and that professionals must act to preserve life rather than diminish it.

Rest's third step calls for the development of a strategy or plan of action (Biggs & Blocker, 1987). How are counselors going to evaluate the ethical aspects of the situations they confront to ensure that they integrate, as part of the counseling process, a sensitivity to the ethical decisions that are involved in the problems of their clients? Counselors need to ensure that they understand and are sensitive to the ethical components in the needs and desires of their clients. These professionals must ensure that when they respond to clients' needs they are fully aware of their own ethical values and that interaction with clients is ethically justifiable in terms of the First- and Second-Order principles. Morally relevant questions need to be asked, questions that tease out the ethical consequences involved in the counseling situation. Where appropriate, counselors need to solicit additional client information so that an informed choice can be made, one that best recognizes and protects the client's rights. In addition, sufficient ethical sophistication is needed so that counselors can resist simplistic justifications and rationalizations for unethical behavior.

The final step in Rest's model involves the process of doing (Biggs & Blocker, 1987). This is the hardest part of being ethical, for not only must we understand the ethical consequences of our behavior, but we must be prepared to act ethically. Many times, by doing what is ethically correct, we may disappoint colleagues and friends, or worse, discover that they have disappointed us. Sometimes doing the right thing will mean a financial loss. Acting on a principle does not come easy, and sometimes does not come cheap. A counselor may lose a client, a friend, or even a job. But the ultimate test of being ethical is being prepared to translate principles into action. This step "involves figuring out the sequence of concrete actions, working around impediments and unexpected difficulties, overcoming fatigue and frustration, resisting distractions and other allurements, and keeping sight of the eventual goal. Perseverance, resoluteness, competence, and 'character' are virtues of Component IV" (Rest, 1984, p. 26).

To be an ethical counselor the professional must first learn his own value system: he must take the time to examine his beliefs and values, and explore where they come from, why they are held, and the strength of his commitment to them. And finally, each counselor must be prepared to act on these beliefs. "Greater moral discursiveness enables us better to understand, listen, respect and respond to other people, however much they differ in culture, class, race, gender, education—or moral convictions" (Ruddick, 1988, p. 49).

REFERENCES

American Psychological Association. 1981. "Ethical Principles of Psychologists," *American Psychologist* **36** (6), 633.

Andre, C. 1987. "What Is Ethics?" *Issues in Ethics* **1** (1), 2.

Biggs, D., and Blocker, D. 1987. *Foundations of Ethical Counseling,* New York: Springer Publishing Co.

Callis, R.; Pope, S. K.; and DePauw, M. E. 1982. *Ethical Standards Casebook,* 3rd ed., Falls Church, American Personnel and Guidance Association.

Chany, W. 1983. *Sourcebook of Chinese Philosophy,* Princeton, N.J.: Princeton University Press.

Donagan, A. 1962. *On the Latter Philosophy of R. G. Collingwood,* Oxford: Oxford University Press.

Edwards, P. (ed.). 1967. *The Encyclopedia of Philosophy,* vol. 1–8, New York: Macmillan.

Etziony, M. D. 1973. *The Physician's Creed,* Springfield, Mass.: Charles C. Thomas, Publisher.

Herman, J. L.; Gartrell, N.; Olarte, S; Feldstein, M.; and Localio, R. 1987. "Psychiatrist-Patient Sexual Contact: Results of a National Survey, II: Psychiatrist's Attitudes," *American Journal of Psychiatry* **144** (2), 168.

Kitchener, K. S. 1984. "Intuition, Critical Evaluation and Ethical Principles: Foundation of Ethical Decisions in Counseling Psychology," *The Counseling Psychologist* **12** (3), 43.

Krutch, J. W. 1959. *Human Nature and the Human Condition,* New York: Random House.

Leader, W. 1976. "Moral Dilemmas Encountered in Psychotherapy." In A. G. Benet (ed.), *Creative Psychotherapy,* La Jolla: California University Associates.

Lippitt, G. L. 1969. *Organizational Renewal,* Englewood Cliffs, N.J.: Prentice Hall.

London, K. 1964. *The Modes and Morals of Psychotherapy,* New York: Holt, Rinehart, and Winston.

Rest, J. 1984. "Research on Moral Development: Implications for Training Psychologists," *The Counseling Psychologist* **12,** 19.

Ruddick, W. 1988. "Ethical Issues in Medical Education: A Philosopher's View," *New York University Physician* **25** (1), 49.

Saad, A. 1988. "Ethical Issues in Medical Education: Why Study Ethics? A Medical Student's View," *New York University Physician* **25** (1), 53.

Spritz, N. 1988. "Control of Life-Prolonging Technology," *New York University Physician,* **45** (1), 24.

Tenneyson, W. W., and Stom, S. M. 1986. "Beyond Professional Standards: Developing Responsibleness," *Journal of Counseling and Development* **64,** 298.

Van Hoose, W. 1980. "Ethics and Counseling," *Counseling and Human Development* **13** (1), 12.

Van Hoose, W., and Kottler, J. 1987. *Ethical and Legal Issues in Counseling and Psychotherapy,* San Francisco: Jossey-Bass Publishers.

Walman, B. 1982. "Ethical Problems in Termination of Psychotherapy." In M. Rosenbaum (ed.), *Ethics and Values in Psychotherapy,* New York: Free Press.

Welfel, E. R., and Lipsitz, N. E. 1983. "Ethical Orientation of Counselors: Its Relationship to Moral Reasoning and Level of Training," *Counselor Education and Supervision* **23** (September): 35.

3

The Rights of the Client

The counselor-client relationship is very much like the relationship that exists between a doctor and a patient or a lawyer and a client. In all three relationships both parties, in our case the client and the counselor, enter into it with certain presumptions and expectations. The client comes to the relationship expecting the counselor to help, in return for which the client is prepared to give up certain things. For example, he is willing to share with the counselor information about his innermost feelings and thoughts. The counselor expects his client to be honest and forthright, to be sincere in what is being said, and to follow the counselor's recommendations. In return, the counselor agrees not to share with anyone else the information he receives in the counseling relationship and, perhaps more importantly, he agrees not to use the information he receives to harm or take advantage of the client. Finally, the counselor agrees to respect and protect the rights of the client.

In this chapter we will look at the rights of the client, beginning with the right of informed consent. In chapter 5 we will examine how the codes of ethics of counseling organizations are designed to protect client rights. In chapter 6 we will take an in-depth look at one of the principle client rights, the right to confidentiality. Let us begin by looking at the concept of informed consent.

INFORMED CONSENT

The following story was reported in the *Buffalo News* in 1988: A forty-three-year-old Seattle sales manager was treated in 1976 for leukemia and recovered. As part of the treatment, the doctors removed his spleen. Two researchers took genetic material from the spleen tissue and through genetic engineering developed a new cell line that proved to be of substantial benefit to cancer victims.

The patient was never told what the researchers were doing with his tissue. In fact, for seven years, he continued to undergo check-ups at the medical center, during which time the researchers continued to take additional specimens. At no time during this period was the patient ever informed of what was happening to his tissues, nor was he ever asked to consent to their use of his tissue for these purposes. Subsequently, the researchers entered into a licensing agreement with a bioengineering firm and pharmaceutical company through which the researchers stood to gain substantially from the royalties realized on their patents.

The patient finally became aware of the activities of these researchers and brought suit, charging that he also should receive royalties from the licenses, since his body and parts thereof, whether inside his body or out, are his property and the researchers had no right to do anything to him (or any part of him) without his prior consent. Since the researchers had failed to receive his prior permission, the reengineered biomaterial continued to be part of him to which he had a property right to recover monies received from the sale thereof (Goodman, 1988, p. C–3).

The California court agreed. It found that "a patient must have the ultimate power to control what becomes of his or her tissues. To hold otherwise would open the door to a massive invasion of human privacy and dignity in the name of medical progress" (Goodman, 1988, p. C–3).

This case should be of interest to the student of counseling ethics for a number of reasons. It is especially instructive because it helps to emphasize how dearly the motion of "informed consent" has come to be held in our society.

What is informed consent and why is it such an important ethical concept for counselors? As California courts have noted, the notion of informed consent evolves from the concepts of privacy and dignity. The notion of privacy, in turn, derives from one of the most fundamental of ethical concepts, the principle of autonomy. Autonomy is defined as the right of an "individual to govern himself according to his own reason" (Grove, 1986, p. 148). We reward and punish individuals for their behavior because we believe that, according to the principle of autonomy, they are responsible for their actions. This means that they have freely chosen to act in the way they have, and could have chosen to act differently if they so desired.

To put it another way, a person makes a decision and, in making this decision, he is at liberty to choose differently. This is what philosophers mean when they say that man has free will. Free will is the freedom to make a choice between alternatives based upon one's own volition, rather than being compelled to act in a manner the individual would not have chosen, or being prevented from acting by the will of another person, state, or authority.

Two necessary conditions must therefore exist in order for there to be free will: the freedom to act and the freedom to choose. If either of these necessary conditions is absent, we do not have free will; consequently, we do not have autonomy. (Freedom of choice also means responsibility and accountability, since the individual could have freely chosen to do something else.)

Ethicists argue that freedom of choice cannot be just any choice, but must in fact be a rational decision by the actor. The actor must have the ability, i.e., the competence, to make a reasoned choice. Rational choice means the ability to understand the consequences of alternative courses of action. Others have argued that a rational choice is more complicated than this. For example, "to the extent that the development of formal operational thinking allows an individual to think about abstract consequences (e.g., death is forever), to think ahead, to think logically about hypothetical possibilities and impossibilities may be one criterion for determining rationality" (Kitchener, 1984, p. 47).

Freedom of action also depends upon being sufficiently informed to make a knowledgeable choice among alternatives. It is here that the issue of informed consent arises. Now what are the elements of informed consent as they pertain to the counselor-client relationship?

First, clients have a right to be told what to expect as best the counselor knows or can anticipate it. Unless clients have the fullest possible knowledge about the situation, interaction will be hindered. The counselor does not have to be clairvoyant, but he does have to be forthcoming and honest.

Second, those who seek counseling have a right to be given the relevant facts regarding potential benefits of therapy as well as the facts regarding potential risks.

Third, clients have a right to be told about alternative courses of treatment and the advantages and disadvantages of choosing one treatment over another. This explanation should be offered in nontechnical language and presented as objectively as possible. It is unethical for counselors to bias their clients' choices by painting one treatment modality in glowing colors while presenting another in a cold and unappealing light.

Fourth, clients should be informed of their rights, including the right to withdraw consent at any time; the right to make a free, uncoerced decision; the right to review their records; the right to know the qualifications of their counselor; the right to know the length of therapy; and the right to know any and all costs involved.

Finally, in order to exercise informed consent, the counselor is obligated to disclose relevant limits (e.g., skills, training, and qualifications) to the client.

These are the rudimentary elements of informed consent. There may be others that apply to a specific situation, such as when clients are used in research. Counselors are advised to be very knowledgeable about the elements of informed consent if they are to ensure that any and all questions and concerns of their clients are addressed. It is no longer acceptable, either ethically or legally, to keep information from clients on the grounds that the subject matter is too technical for them to understand. Today clients clearly have a right to know information about themselves and to control what will happen to them within the counseling environment. In the classic words of Justice Cardozo, "Every human being of adult years and sound mind has a right to determine what shall be done with his own body" (Slovenko, 1973, p. 406).

The members of the Committee on Privacy and Confidentiality of the California State Psychological Association collaborated on a set of sample documents, including a statement of client rights, an initial contract form, and an informed consent form. These statements are reproduced here in the hope that counselors will consider adopting similar statements for use in private practice.

Client's Rights Statement

This statement begins with the therapist's professional qualifications, including (at a minimum) name, office address, and telephone number, highest relevant degree, and certification or license number. The sentences that follow suggest what a client's basic rights in psychotherapy ought to include:

1. "You have the right to decide *not* to receive psychotherapy from me; if you wish, I shall provide you with the names of other qualified psychotherapists.

2. "You have the right to end therapy at any time without any moral, legal, or financial obligations.

3. "You have the right to ask any questions about the procedures used during therapy; if you wish, I shall explain my usual methods to you.

4. "You have the right to prevent the use of certain therapeutic techniques; I shall inform you of my intention to use any unusual procedures and shall describe any risks involved.

5. "You have the right to prevent electronic recording of any part of the therapy session; permission to record must be granted by you in writing on a form that explains exactly what is to be done and for what period of time. I shall explain my intended use of the recordings and provide a written statement to the effect that they will not be used for any other purpose; you have the right to withdraw your permission to record at any time.

6. "You have the right to review your records in the files at any time.

7. "One of your most important rights involves confidentiality: Within certain limits, information revealed by you during therapy will be kept strictly confidential and *will not be revealed* to any other person or agency *without your written permission.*

8. "If you request it, any part of your records in the files can be released to any person or agencies you designate. I shall tell you, at the time, whether or not I think making the record public will be harmful to you.

9. "You should also know that there are certain situations in which, as a psychotherapist, I am required *by law* to reveal information obtained during therapy to other persons or agencies—*without your permission.* Also, I am not required to inform you of my actions in this regard. These situations are as follows: (a) If you threaten grave bodily harm or death to another person, I am required by law to inform the intended victim and appropriate law enforcement agencies; (b) if a court of law issues a legitimate subpoena, I am required by law to provide the information specifically described by the subpoena; (c) if you are in therapy or being tested by order of a court of law, the results of the treatment or tests ordered must be revealed to the court."

Initial Contract Form

1. "I agree to enter into psychotherapy with (name of therapist) for (number negotiated) one-hour sessions during the next (number negotiated) weeks.

2. "I agree to pay (amount negotiated) for each completed one-hour therapy session. Payment will be made by me or by a third party when billed.

3. "I understand that I can leave therapy at any time and that I have no moral, legal, or financial obligation to complete the maximum number of sessions listed in this contract; I am contracting to pay only for completed therapy sessions."

Both client and therapist should sign and date this form.

Informed Consent Form

"Psychotherapy may involve the risk of remembering unpleasant events and can arouse intense emotions of fear and anger. Intense feelings of anxiety, depression, frustration, loneliness, or helplessness may also be aroused.

"The benefits from psychotherapy may be that you will be better able to handle or cope with your family or other social relationships, thus experiencing more satisfaction from those relationships. Another possible benefit may be a better understanding of your personal goals and values; this may lead to greater maturity and growth as a person.

"You should know that a psychologist is not a physician and cannot prescribe or provide you with any drugs or medication or perform any medical procedures. If medical treatment is indicated, I can recommend a physician for you or you can choose any physician whom you wish to see.

"If you wish to receive psychotherapy from (name of therapist), please sign your name below."

Client then signs and dates this form. (Everstine et al., 1980, p. 832)

One of the elements assumed in the counseling relationship is the right of the client to a competent counselor.

WHAT IS COMPETENCE?

Webster's Unabridged Dictionary defines "competent" as "1. answering all requirements; suitable; fit; convenient; hence, sufficient; fit for the purpose; adequate; as a competent force: 2. having ability or capacity; duly qualified; as, a competent workman" (Grove, 1986, p. 463).

Competence is one of those concepts with which all professional organizations struggle. What are the standards by which the competent behavior of a counselor is to be measured? How can justification be offered for declaring a counselor's actions "incompetent"? One of the problems in determining what constitutes competence is that there is no objective standard by which a counselor's ability can be measured. Professionals, unlike blue-collar workers, cannot be judged by the number of widgets they produce per hour. Time and motion studies cannot be performed to determine how long it should take a counselor to (re)solve a client's particular problem. This is because counselors, unlike factory employees, work with that infinite variable known as the human being. Since human beings differ, each person's problems are likely to be different as well. Therefore, it is almost impossible to agree upon an objective set of standards for judging counselors. Assessment tends, then, to be relegated to the realm of the subjective and the qualitative.

Here again, there is a major difference between being "competent" and being "good." While counselors ought to strive to be outstanding in their respective fields, there is a vast range of behaviors that falls within the acceptable limits of competence, the lower limit of which has been called "marginally competent," in some texts—that is, behavior that just falls above the line of being incompetent. The mid-range is termed "good," while exceptional abilities are frequently termed "model" or "outstanding." The standard of measure is further complicated because it is very apparent to the professional in any field that incompetence is more than unacceptable. Incompetent practices expose the counselor to the possibility of termination and civil liability for malpractice.

The issue of competence is still further complicated by the tension existing between unions and employers on the question of where to draw the line. The unions' purpose is to represent the best interests of their members; therefore, they tend to draw the line of competence as low as possible so as to give their members the maximum range of freedom in acting as professionals. Management, on the other hand, would like to draw the line as high as possible in order to serve the best interest of the clients and to minimize complaints about poor behavior on the part of employees.

Issues of competence are usually resolved by asking members of a profession to determine if they would have acted the same given the same set of circumstances. If the colleagues conclude that their conduct would have been the same as the professional in question, then what they are saying is that the counselor's behavior conformed to at least a minimum standard of competence. On the other hand, if they determine that they would have reacted differently, in a sense they would be saying that the counselor's behavior fell below the minimum standards. We term this the "reasonable man" standard; that is, "What would a reasonable person similarly situated do?" This has generally become the way by which professional competence is determined, by the testimony of one's peers.

The National Academy of Certified Clinical Mental Health Counselors is one organization whose code of ethics is helping professionals to address the question of competence. Principal 2, entitled "Competence," reads as follows:

> The maintenance of high standards of professional competence is a responsibility shared by all clinical mental health counselors in the interest of the public and the profession as a whole. Clinical mental health counselors recognize the boundaries of their competence and the limitations of their techniques and only provide services, use techniques, or offer opinions as professionals that meet recognized standards. Throughout their careers, clinical mental health counselors maintain knowledge of professional information related to the services they render.
>
> a. Clinical mental health counselors accurately represent their competence, education, training, and experience.
>
> b. As teachers, clinical mental health counselors perform their duties based on careful preparation so that their instruction is accurate, up-to-date, and scholarly.
>
> c. Clinical mental health counselors recognize the need for continuing training to prepare themselves to serve persons of all ages and cultural backgrounds. They are open to new procedures and sensitive to differences between groups of people and changes in expectations and values over time.
>
> d. Clinical mental health counselors with the responsibility for decisions involving individuals or policies based on test results should know and understand literature relevant to the tests used and testing problems with which they deal.

e. Clinical mental health counselors/practitioners recognize that their effectiveness depends in part upon their ability to maintain sound interpersonal relations, and that temporary or more enduring aberrations on their part may interfere with their abilities or distort their appraisals of others. Therefore, they refrain from undertaking any activity in which the personal problems are likely to lead to inadequate professional services or harm to a client; or, if they are already engaged in such activity when they become aware of their personal problems, they would seek competent professional assistance to determine whether they should suspend or terminate services to one or all of their clients. (Callis et al., 1982, p. 174)

Some states have also attempted to address this question of competence on the part of members of the helping professions. A good example is the work of the State of Tennessee in developing standards by which they measure the competence of their school counselors. These standards, set forth in the Tennessee Career Ladder Better Schools program, include the following:

I.   Plans for Delivery of Counseling, Guidance and Services.

   A. Establishes appropriate goals consistent with the programs of the school system.

   B. Prepares plans and materials for counseling, career development, educational and information services.

   C. Assists in planning programs related to counseling and guidance for staff and parents.

II. Delivers Effective Counseling and Guidance Services.

   A. Counsels learners, individually and in groups, in regard to their personal-social, educational, and/or career needs.

   B. Works with school staff to provide school life/counseling guidance programs.

   C. Provides effective career development, educational and informational services.

   D. Establishes and maintains appropriate counselor behavior.

   E. Establishes and maintains a climate conducive to the personal and academic growth of students.

III. Uses Evaluation to Improve Counseling/Guidance Services and School-Wide Instruction.

A. Uses information about learner performance to improve school-wide instruction.

B. Reports learner status and progress to teachers, learners, and parents.

C. Evaluates all services/programs provided to learners, teachers, and parents.

IV. Manages Counseling/Guidance Programs Effectively.

A. Maintains an ongoing counseling/guidance program in cooperation with other school staff.

B. Makes effective use of resources.

V. Establishes and Maintains a Professional Leadership Role.

A. Improves professional skills and knowledge.

B. Takes a leadership role in improving education.

C. Serves as a liaison for home, school, and community.

D. Performs professional responsibilities efficiently.

VI. Communicates Effectively.

A. Writes clearly and correctly.

B. Writes professionally relevant literature/material with comprehension. (Tennessee Career Ladder Better Schools Program, 1986, pp. 12–18)

No discussion of competence would be complete without considering one last, and perhaps the most vexing, question: Whose responsibility is it to weed out incompetent counselors from the ranks of the counseling profession? Recently a group of counselors in two upstate New York counties were asked to respond to ten questions about competence. Sixty-four percent of the respondents indicated that they were aware of a colleague whom they would judge to be an incompetent counselor. The colleague's incompetence was evident to the respondents' staff as well, thus giving the profession a bad name and drawing attention away from the good work being done by competent counselors. Generally, the incompetent colleagues were viewed as being "carried" by the administration until it was time for them to retire.

The presence of ethical standards in various helping professional organizations places an obligation on the membership to report incompetent behavior of colleagues. For example, the American Personnel Guidance Association (APGA) Ethical Standards state, "A.3. Ethical behavior among professional associates, both members and nonmembers, must be expected at all times. When information is possessed that raises doubt as to the ethical behavior of professional colleagues, whether Association members or not, the member must take action to attempt to rectify such a condition. Such action shall use the institution's channels first, and then use procedures established by the State branch, division, or association" (Callis, 1982, p. 9). It is important to note that all organizations in the helping professions conclude that incompetence on the part of their members is a violation of the ethical codes of those associations.

One of the best ways to ensure competence is by understanding and respecting the rights of clients. It is now time to reflect on these rights.

THE CLIENT BILL OF RIGHTS

The codes of ethical standards for professional counseling organizations (see chapter 5) are designed to govern and set limits on the conduct of their respective members. These codes serve as general statements of professional obligations rather than setting forth a client's "bill of rights." I believe that the counselor will benefit from a more focused guide to good practice, one that is cast from the perspective of a basic list of fundamental rights.

A number of authors have identified the various rights of clients (Kottler & Vriend, 1975; Haley, 1976; Koch & Koch, 1976; Parloff, 1976; Berger, 1982; Corey, Corey & Callanan, 1979; Van Hoose & Kottler, 1987). Among the rights they have included are:

1. The right to equal treatment. The right not to be treated differently from other clients because of race, age, sex, religion, national origin, handicap, sexual preference, physical attractiveness, socioeconomic status, or presenting conditions (Van Hoose & Kottler 1987).

2. The right to expect that the counselor will act to promote the client's good and minimize harm to the client.

3. The right to expect that the client's concerns, no matter how frivolous they may appear, will be taken seriously by the counselor.

4. The right to expect that the counselor's highest priority is the welfare of his client.

5. The right to expect that the counseling relations will be constructive and not destructive (Martin, 1976).

6. The right to expect that the counselor will respect and act to promote and protect the rights of his client.

7. The right to informed consent.

8. The right to have what is said in the counseling relationship held in the strictest of confidence and to be told in advance of any limitations on the counselor's right to maintain confidence (Corey, Corey & Callanan, 1979).

9. The right to have a clear understanding of all costs before the therapeutic relationship commences. Where appropriate, the right to reasonable assistance in obtaining third party payment and, when necessary, reasonable accommodation through a deferred payment plan (Corey, Corey & Callanan, 1984).

10. The right to know about the competence of the counselor. The client should be informed of the counselor's training, including any specialized training, degrees, certificate, and license. The client should be informed if an intern or a para-professional will be included in the counseling relationship, the role they will play, and provisions for supervision (Corey, Corey & Callanan, 1984), as well as prior experience with similar clients and the results.

11. Clients involved in psychotherapy have a right to learn as much about the treatment as possible, including, but not limited to, "a description of the plan of action individually designed for the particular case, including the specific rationale for any intervention attempted" (Van Hoose & Kottler, 1987, p. 160).

12. The client also has a right to know any diagnosis, to participate significantly in the development of the treatment modality, to be consulted about any proposed modification in treatment, and to assist in establishing the short- and long-term therapeutic goals (Van Hoose & Kottler, 1987).

13. Clients have the right to have all explanations conveyed in plain English. Counselors should carefully explain all technical jargon in simple terms.

14. The right to expect that the counseling profession will maintain the highest standards by policing the conduct of its members.

15. The right to grieve the unethical conduct of a counselor and to have an expeditious and fair hearing without risking embarrassment, ridicule, and unwarranted invasion of privacy.

16. A client has the right not to be abused by the counselor. This right includes freedom from physical (including sexual) and psychological abuse.

REFERENCES

Berger, M. 1982. "Ethical Problems in the Use of Videotape." In M. Rosenbaum (ed.), *Ethics and Values in Psychotherapy: A Guidebook,* New York: Free Press.

Callis, R.; Pope, S. K.; and DePauw, M. E. 1982. *Ethical Standards Casebook,* Falls Church, Va.: American Personnel and Guidance Association.

Corey, G.; Corey, M. S.; and Callanan, P. 1984. *Issues and Ethics in the Helping Professions,* 2nd ed., Monterey, Calif.: Brooks/Cole Publishing. First edition, 1979; third edition, 1988.

Everstine, L.; Everstin, D. S.; Heymann, G. M.; True, R. H.; Frey, D. H.; Johnson, H. G.; and Seiden, R. H. 1980. "Privacy and Confidentiality in Psychotherapy," *American Psychologist* **35** (9), 828.

Goodman, E. Op-Ed Column, *The Buffalo News,* July 29, 1988, C–3.

Grove, P. G. 1986. *Webster's Third New International Dictionary,* Springfield, Mass.: Merriam-Webster, Inc.

Haley, J. 1976. *Problem-Solving Therapy,* New York: Harper & Row.

Kitchener, K. S. 1984. "Institutions, Critical Evaluation, and Ethical Decisions in Counseling Psychology," *The Counseling Psychologist* **12** (3), 41.

Koch, J., and Koch, L. 1976. "A Consumer's Guide to Therapy for Couples," *Psychiatry Today* **9** (10), 33.

Kottler, J. A., and Vriend, J. 1975. "How Good Is Your Shrink?" *Detroit Discovery* (Spring), 12.

Martin, M. E. 1976. *Report from the Study Group on Legal Concerns of the Rehabilitation Counselor,* Stout: University of Wisconsin: Stout Research and Training Center.

Parloff, M. B. "Shopping for the Right Therapy," *Saturday Review,* February 12, 18.

Slovenko, R. 1973. *Psychiatry and Law,* Boston: Little, Brown, and Company.

Tennessee Career Ladder Better Schools Program. 1986. *Counselor Orientation Manual,* Nashville: Tennessee State Department of Education.

Van Hoose, W. H., and Kottler, J. A. 1987. *Ethical and Legal Issues in Counseling and Psychotherapy,* San Francisco, Calif.: Jossey-Bass.

4

The Rights of the Counselor

Volumes of material have been produced on the rights of the client. In fact, much of this book is devoted to that very subject, either directly or indirectly, through a discussion of the duties and obligations of the counselor. Unfortunately, precious little has been written on the rights of the counselor. This chapter looks at those rights from two perspectives: first, the private life versus the public life of the counselor; and second, the rights of the counselor as a professional. The approach taken here is to rely heavily on case studies to delineate the issues involved, with subsequent discussion provided to clarify the salient points and to identify the principles of those issues.

One salient feature of professionalism is concern about the behavior of individual members at those points where professional life and private life intersect. Jurisdiction over the private ethical conduct of a profession's members is usually asserted through a principle that recognizes the inherent rights of private conduct, but asserts jurisdiction when the professional's private life reflects negatively on him or the profession generally. The principle usually takes one of two forms: either an obligation not to let personal problems interfere with professional conduct, or a duty not to act publicly in a manner so as to denigrate the image of the profession in the public's eyes. Examples of these principles can be seen in the American Psychological Association's Ethics Principles 3 and 2.f. To quote Principle

3: "Psychologists' moral and ethical standards of behavior are a personal matter to the same degree as they are for any other citizen, except as these may compromise the fulfillment of their professional responsibilities or reduce the public trust in psychology and psychologists. Regarding their own behavior, psychologists are sensitive to prevailing community standards and to the possible impact that conformity to or deviation from these standards may have upon the quality of their performance as psychologists. Psychologists are also aware of the possible impact of their public behavior on the ability of colleagues to perform their professional duties" (APA, 1981, p. 634).

Principle 2.f. states that, "Psychologists recognize that personal problems and conflicts may interfere with their professional effectiveness. Accordingly, they refrain from undertaking any activity in which their personal problems are likely to lead to inadequate performance or harm to a client, colleague, student, or research participant. If engaged in such activity when they become aware of their personal problems, they seek competent professional assistance to determine whether they should suspend, terminate, or limit the scope of their professional and/or scientific activities" (APA, 1981, p. 634). Let's look at how these principles are applied in a few hypothetical cases.

COUNSELORS ARE PEOPLE, TOO

Imagine the following scenario: It's Monday morning, you have had a tough weekend, you would love to get another hour's sleep, but that's impossible. In fact, unless you hurry you will be late for work. You look down, and you discover that your new puppy has decided to spend the night teething on your brand new pair of shoes. These were the shoes that you worked so hard to find; that fit so perfectly; that, when you bought them, you said you would never be able to find another pair just like them. They are now ruined. What a way to start a Monday morning.

You go downstairs to make breakfast. You are outraged to discover that you are out of coffee. There isn't even instant coffee lying around in the corner of the refrigerator. You know you can't start your day without your morning cup of coffee. Now you are really beginning to steam.

You get in the car and head off to work. While waiting for a traffic light to change, just around the corner from the office, the driver behind you isn't paying attention and inadvertently plows into the back of your car. Now you have to pull over, find insurance forms, wait for the police, and then fill out all kinds of forms. By the time you are done, you are late for work. All you can think about is getting to the office, calling your insurance company, and starting to make the arrangements to get your car fixed. As you walk in the door, you notice that your first appointment is on time. You walk by him. You say, "I'll be right with you," walk into your office, close the door, sit down at your desk, and decide how to proceed.

Clearly, for the moment, all you can think of is calling your insurance company and getting the accident processed. But you have a client waiting. Should you (1) cancel the appointment; (2) start the session immediately, but end it early so you can get on with your telephone calls; (3) tell your client that you are going to need about ten minutes to get your wits together and to make some phone calls because you have been involved in a minor traffic accident on the way to work? What is the right thing to do? If you cancel the session, are you being fair to your client? Maybe your client really needs to see you today, or has traveled a great distance at considerable personal inconvenience to meet with you. To be sure, it would be wonderful to have a whole hour to straighten out your personal affairs, but do you need the whole hour? It is a question of balancing your professional responsibility to your client and your own personal needs.

The second option, abbreviating the session, appears to satisfy the responsibility to your client. With an abbreviated session you should be able to end the session early enough to make those calls to the insurance company before your next client arrives. But can you really give your fullest attention to the client's needs even during the abbreviated session? Wouldn't it be easier to get your problems addressed first so you could approach the session with nothing on your mind other than your client's problems and concerns? Is there anything wrong with saying to your client, "Listen, I had a small problem on the way to work, and I am going to need about ten minutes to get the matter straightened out. How about having that second cup of coffee, and I will be with you shortly." This is probably what would happen in any other situation or any other profession. Counselors often have trouble accepting that they are persons, too. As with other people in the helping professions, clients view counselors as being slightly more than perfect despite all efforts by counselors to disabuse them of that notion.

This is not only true in situations where the counselor has had a bad day, but also in situations where clients see their counselor outside the work context. For example, maybe you wear a sportcoat and tie to work everyday. One Saturday, attired in jeans, you meet your client in the local K-Mart. Your client is shocked to discover that you have any clothes other than that sportcoat and tie.

Let us consider another scene. You work as a counselor in a substance abuse rehabilitation center. Saturday night, you go to the local bar for a few drinks with your friends. Coming out of the bar you meet the parents of your client, who are amazed to see you in a place like that. Again what is the responsibility to your client in terms of being a role model, setting a good example, living the good life versus your right to be a person and to have a life outside the clinic?

Gifts

Imagine the following: You are a school counselor and you have worked hard to raise the sights of a particular female student in your school. She had very low aspirations and felt that she should play it safe and apply to a college to which she felt she had a reasonable chance of getting admitted. You worked with this student and accomplished two things. First, you improved the quality of her application and, second, you convinced her that she ought to try for the best school to which she had even the remotest chance of being admitted. As things turn out, she applies to Harvard and is notified in February of her senior year that she has been admitted. Her parents are grateful. One morning when you come to work you find a bottle of your favorite liquor on your desk with a "Thank you" note from her parents. What do you do? Do you accept the liquor and write a little note back saying it was all in a day's work, but that you appreciate their gratitude? Do you send the liquor back with a note saying that as a matter of policy you do not accept gifts; that what you did for their daughter was part of your job and you receive ample remuneration from the school district? What do you do?

I described this case in one of my classes. Most of the students felt it was appropriate to accept the gift. After all, everyone is familiar with situations in grade school where parents send a little end-of-the-year gift as a thank-you to their child's teacher.

Now, let us change our hypothetical case slightly. We begin with the same scenario: You help the young lady raise her sights, she applies to Harvard, is accepted, and her parents are grateful. Her parents wish to express their gratitude. Instead of sending you a bottle of liquor that costs about ten dollars, you come to work one morning and find an envelope on your desk with a ten dollar bill inside the same appreciative note. Now what do you do? Do you accept the money and express your thanks? Or do you send the money back with a note saying that you were simply doing your job and, while you appreciate their gratitude, you make it a practice not to accept gifts. What do you do?

When I raised this hypothetical case study in class, more students felt that it was inappropriate to accept money than felt it was inappropriate to accept the liquor. What was offensive about the money that was not also offensive about a gift?

Let us take the same situation one last time. The facts are the same except in this case you get a gift of chocolate. As it turns out, it is a five-pound box of Godiva chocolate that costs about fifty dollars. What do you do? Again, the class reacted differently. A number of the students refused the gift, arguing that it was the amount of money that was at issue.

But I ask you, what is the issue? Is it the cost of the gift, is it the nature of the gift, or is it taking a gift at all?

This little exercise will help you clarify your own values. Will you accept a gift from someone for doing your job? Do you feel guilty if you do? Do you feel less guilty if the gift is in some form other than money, for example, liquor or a mongrammed towel? Do you feel more guilty if the gift is expensive rather than inexpensive? After all, a gift is a gift. Should there be a magic threshold beyond which a gift is inappropriate? More importantly, does accepting a gift have consequences for your future relationship with your client? Does accepting the gift compromise your freedom to act according to your ethical principles? Are you creating false expectations? For example, don't gift givers have the right to assume special treatment because they have given you an extra payment? It is important to understand the ethical consequences of accepting a gift from a client *before* you accept it. After you accept a gift, it may be too late. In fact, the very codes that seem to be so stringent in other places are strangely silent on the question of the appropriateness of a counselor accepting a gift.

Commercialism

As society becomes increasingly more conscious of both its mental and physical health, there is greater opportunity and temptation for counselors to engage in commercial activities. The opportunities include product endorsements, talk show appearances, newspaper columns, and the like. Such well-known personalities as Sonja Freeman, Joyce Brothers, and Ruth Westheimer come to mind here. Counselors who engage in commercial activities run the risk of inadvertently abusing their position, violating their clients' rights and denigrating the image of the profession in the public's eye.

What are the ethical issues that arise when counselors engage in such activities, and what are the permissible parameters for such activities? Let's look at three cases cited by the American Psychological Association.

[Case 1:] Several psychologists wrote to the Ethics Committee to complain about an APA member who was appearing on radio and TV talk shows with a number of her clients, all of whom were well-known stars in the entertainment industry. In the talk show format the psychologist encouraged her clients, some of whom had terminated treatment, others of whom were still active clients, to talk about their reasons for seeking treatment and their experiences in therapy. The complainants argued that the program clearly violated the psychologist-client confidentiality principle, especially principle 5.a., because it was not professional, disclosed the identity of clients, and revealed details of treatment. In response to the Ethics Committee inquiry, the psychologist revealed that her clients themselves had suggested the show. She had thoroughly discussed the pros and cons of self-disclosure with them, and all had agreed that the benefits to the general public of their self-disclosure outweighed any risk involved. The psychologist had obtained written, informed consent agreements, and all the clients were willing to provide statements to attest to what had transpired. (APA, 1987, p. 70)

It is not unethical, a priori, for counselors to engage in commercial activities. The problem is that such activities come dangerously close to violating the ethical principles of their cognizant professional organization. Public appearances by counselors put these professionals in the delicate position of wanting to say enough to be interesting to the audience, while on the other hand respecting the privacy rights of their clients. Talk show hosts push their guests in the direction of being provocative and sensational. Counselors need to understand in the clearest terms that, when they participate in talk shows, control of the show rests in the hands of the host. Even the most highly trained and experienced guest may regret a casual remark made under the glare of television lights in response to what appeared at the time to be an innocent question from a very skilled interviewer.

If counselors wish to appear on talk shows, they need to demand of the host and producer the same level of informed consent that they provide their clients. There needs to be a clear agreement on all the ground rules before the counselor ever steps foot on stage. This agreement should include the role of the counselor, examples of questions to be asked, acknowledgment of what the counselor is willing or unwilling to discuss, the names of other people who may be appearing with the counselor, the purpose of the show, and so on. If the talk show producer is not prepared to agree to these terms, then the counselor is strongly encouraged to decline the opportunity for a moment of fame that may, in the end, turn out to be a monumental mistake.

Fortunately for our counselor in the present case, the Ethics Committee (APA, 1987) found insufficient grounds to conclude that the ethical principles of the APA had been violated.

Our second case involves the promotion of an unorthodox treatment with guaranteed results.

[Case 2:] Two psychologists claimed in their advertisements that they had achieved a startling breakthrough in developing a new and unique therapeutic technique (APA, 1987). They asserted that the treatment provided "profound and surprising" insights into behavior and produced clients who "actually get well," even clients whom other therapists had been unable to help. Calling themselves the "George Washington and Abraham Lincoln" of a revolutionary new mode of psychotherapy, they appeared on radio and television talk shows and presented many public seminars on help and self-help. They placed advertisements making substantially the same claims in the local newspapers and nationally circulated magazines. In their public statements and promotional material, they claimed to be "myth busters" and cited glowing testimonials to their work from authors of fiction and nonfiction books that dealt with psychological themes.

In response to the Ethics Committee inquiry, the pair explained that they had used the new treatment mode in their joint private practice for more than five years and were well satisfied by its efficacy (APA, 1987). Unable to indicate any research that supported their claims for successful treatment, the psychologists explained that they had thought it more important to get the word out on an effective treatment than to waste time on laboratory exercises that could only, at best, simulate the therapeutic situation. Moreover, they argued that the hyperbolic tone of their advertisements and appearances was simply the way of public performance and promotion. One could not expect the public to have the patience to try to interpret the monotonous and unnecessarily obscure jargon of the profession. (APA, 1987, pp. 57-58)

The Ethics Committee determined that the behavior of these psychologists was akin to the snake oil salesmen of the wild West. Their overall behavior was characterized as being unprofessional. In the words of the committee, "the advertisements used by these psychologists to promote their books and public lectures were neither professional, scientifically acceptable, nor factually informative. Rather, sensational statements and unsupported claims were made, rendering the advertisements classic examples of unprofessional behavior and gross exaggeration and, therefore, clear violations of Principle 4.e." (APA, 1987, p. 58).

Counselors have the right to promote their successes provided they can scientifically document their claims. The public puts great faith in the words of a professional. It is easy for society to be duped by the unscrupulous con artist masquerading in the clothing of a professional. Therefore, professional organizations demand accountability for claims made by their members. Counselors should take extra care to ensure that their claims can be substantiated by empirical data and can be independently reproduced and verified.

A good rule of thumb is to ask a colleague to react to any claim you may wish to make. See if your colleague feels comfortable with your assertion. If reservations are expressed, see if there is a better way to say what you want to say without raising the specter of acting unethically.

Our final case concerns the endorsement of products. Few will ever find themselves in the position of achieving such status that their personal endorsement of a product will help the sales of that product. This case is offered not because counselors are expected to be called upon to endorse sports equipment, but to suggest, in an admittedly exaggerated way, that people often take the word of professionals far too seriously. A counselor involved in diet control and behavior modification may very well be asked by a client to recommend exercise equipment. Counselors are frequently asked to recommend other professionals, especially attorneys. When this happens, the client assumes, rightfully, that the persons being recommended must be competent because they have been endorsed by the counselor.

[Case 3:] A leading industrial/organizational psychologist became well known among the general public after his book on aggression in athletes became a best seller. Psychologist Q appeared on talk shows and was extensively interviewed in the press during the promotion campaign set up by his publisher. His tan, rugged appearance and irreverent wit made him popular with audiences.

The advertising agency that handled the account of a major tennis equipment manufacturer, taking note of the attractive image the psychologist had so quickly developed, asked him to endorse their products in a series of magazine advertisements. He agreed, and the advertisements appeared in several magazines with national circulation, featuring his photograph and identifying him specifically as an industrial/organizational psychologist. The ad quoted him as stating that, as a psychologist, he found that using this tennis equipment had improved his game.

Informed by several APA members that the advertisement had appeared, the Ethics Committee in turn notified the psychologist that he had committed an apparent violation of principle 4.f. of the *Ethical Principles.* In response, the psychologist pleaded ignorance of this section of the ethics code (APA, 1987, pp. 58-59).

Principle 4.f. of the Ethics Code of the American Psychological Association states that, "Psychologists do not participate for personal gain in commercial announcements or advertisements recommending to the public the purchase or use of proprietary or single source products or services when that participation is based solely upon their identification as psychologists" (APA, 1981, p. 635). The committee found that ignorance is no defense and that his behavior violated the ethics code.

Substance Abuse

We would like to think that counselors are less prone to the ravaging effects of substance abuse because many see the consequences in the practice of their profession. Unfortunately, the statistics demonstrate the contrary to be true.

Let us look at two case studies where the substance being abused is alcohol.

[Case 1:] A former research assistant charged Psychologist D, principal investigator for a major research project, with falsely accusing and subsequently firing the complainant for failure to perform her work assignments. The complainant claimed that Psychologist D had alcohol problems so serious that he was inebriated on the job and frequently forgot instructions he had issued the day before. The complainant also alleged that her supervisor had become so irrational in his behavior as to jeopardize the research project. The research assistant concluded that she had been unfairly fired, and that Psychologist D should be prevented from continuing his tenure as principal investigator for the sake of others employed on the project, whose dissertations depended on the timely and proper completion of the research.

The Ethics Committee's initial letter to Psychologist D was not answered. Psychologist D's secretary, however, replied on his behalf to the second letter. She indicated that he was in the hospital and would reply to the charges upon his recovery, which was expected in a month. Several weeks later, during which time the Committee made contingency plans to contact the department head, Psychologist D responded and threw himself on the mercy of the Committee. He admitted to a drinking problem. Although he had recognized it himself at the onset of organic symptoms, he had been unable either to control his drinking or seek professional help. He had eventually had an automobile accident while intoxicated, in which he wrecked his car and hurt himself, but fortunately injured no one else. His month in the hospital forced him to stop drinking. Now that he was released and mending, he felt that he could abstain from drinking and rectify the mistake he made. He had, in fact, initiated the reinstatement of the complainant, and submitted a copy of his correspondence with the department head to that effect (APA, 1987, pp. 38–39).

The Ethics Committee determined that Psychologist D had violated principle 2.f. of the Ethical Code of the American Psychological Association which, as mentioned earlier, states, "Psychologists recognize that personal problems and conflicts may interfere with professional effectiveness. Accordingly, they refrain from undertaking any activities in which their personal problems are likely to lead to inadequate performance or harm to a client, colleague, student, or research participant. If engaged in such activity, when they become aware of the personal problems, they seek competent professional assistance to determine whether they should suspend, terminate, or limit the scope of their professional and/or scientific activities" (APA, 1981, p. 634).

The Committee recommended that "Psychologist D be censured with the stipulation that he enroll in a monitored treatment program for his alcoholism and furnish the Committee with a plan for the appropriate supervision of his professional activities. He accepted the censure and complied with the stipulation. The case was closed" (APA, 1987, p. 39).

[Case 2:] An attorney engaged the services of Psychologist L to bolster the defense of her client, a seventeen-year-old boy accused of sexually molesting a much younger boy. The accused teenager's upbringing was extremely disturbed, he himself had been abused physically and sexually as a young child. The defense attorney asked Psychologist L to testify to the often devastating impact that early abuse may have on a child's development, in the hope that the presiding judge would order the boy to receive psychological services rather than sentence him to incarceration.

Psychologist L appeared at the stipulated time to testify, but in an obviously inebriated condition. The shocked attorney was unable to obtain a postponement, so the psychologist was called to the stand. Though he managed to stumble through his testimony, his condition was apparent to all in the courtroom as he visibly swayed and staggered leaving the witness stand. Later the judge in the case cautioned the jury to disregard Psychologist L's testimony on the ground that his condition invalidated his oath.

The defense attorney filed a complaint with the Ethics Committee, pointing out the damage done to her client and to the image of psychologists within the local legal community. When the Ethics Committee contacted Psychologist L, he replied that he was deeply remorseful and pained by what had occurred. He had become so anxious about his first court appearance that he had taken a drink to calm himself down and, unaccustomed to hard liquor, had utterly misjudged the effect it would have. He asked the Committee for forgiveness for his mistake, observing that it was a first offense and would never occur again. (APA, 1987, p. 41)

The Committee found Psychologist L guilty of violating General Principle 3, in that he behaved in a way that denigrated the image of psychology and psychologists in the public's eye.

THE UMBRELLA OF PROFESSIONALISM

When are counselors off duty? Are counselors, like policemen, on duty twenty-four hours a day? Are counselors like the principal who lived in the neighborhood of her school and felt obligated to get formally dressed when she shopped in the local supermarket because she was certain to meet pupils and their parents and it was important to maintain the image of a principal at all times? The following case is an example of a professional who still falls within the jurisdiction of the Codes of Ethics, even though the behavior in question did not occur while he was working as a counselor. While you may wish to argue with the conclusions of the Ethics Committee, the case is illustrative because it points out the Ethics Committee's opinion of the broad dimensions of an individual's obligations to act according to the ethical principles of the profession.

[Case 1:] The president of a major land grant college, Psychologist E, refused to approve the promotion of Dr. W, a female geologist, to associate professor, despite positive recommendations from Dr. W's department and from the faculty senate committee. However, in the same round of personnel decisions, he approved the promotion of Dr. P, a male chemist, to associate professor. Dr. P's record of scholarship and professional recognition in chemistry was comparable with Dr. W's accomplishments in geology.

At the suggestion of a colleague in the university psychology department, Dr. W submitted a complaint to the Ethics Committee. Psychologist E responded—after a second communication from the Ethics office—that the Ethics Committee had no jurisdiction over the situation because it concerned his work as a university president, not as a psychologist. He insisted that there were no distinctions between the qualifications between Dr. W and Dr. P, but that he was not free to discuss the details of university personnel decisions with those outside the process. (APA, 1987, p. 45)

The Ethics Committee found Psychologist E guilty of violating the preamble of the Ethical Principles of the American Psychological Association for failing to respond in a timely manner and for failing to recognize their jurisdiction in this matter by fully cooperating with the inquiry. For this offense they censured him. The preamble states, "Psychologists cooperate with duly constituted committees of the American Psychological Association, in particular the Ethics Committee, by responding promptly and completely" (APA, 1981, p. 633). They also found that his denial of Dr. W's promotion to associate professor was based upon sexual discrimination, a violation of Principle 3.b. of the Code of Ethics. The Ethics Committee asserted that as long as he was a psychologist *and* a member of the American Psychological Association, his conduct as an employee or employer must conform to the ethical standards of the Association, even when not engaged in the practice of psychology.

Society expects members of professional organizations to serve by example. We expect lawyers to be law-abiding citizens, we expect doctors not to smoke, we expect substance abuse counselors not to get drunk or be arrested for possession of a controlled substance. Similarly, clients and the general public expect sex therapists to have exemplary sex lives, marriage counselors not to be divorced, and family therapists not to have domestic problems. Thus, there may be times when actions in their personal lives are judged by the same ethical standards as behavior in their professional lives.

Recommendations

1. Know and understand the ethical principles of the organization that governs your counseling speciality.

2. Act ethically at all times in your personal, public, professional, and private life.

3. Consult a colleague when you feel you are confronting a problematic ethical situation.

4. Write to the Ethics Committee of your professional organization for advice on how you ought to proceed in situations which you feel are marginally ethical. For example, if you plan to engage in a novel commercial activity, have been asked to promote a product, write a column for a local newspaper, and so forth, seek an opinion on the professional ethics of the venture before embarking on your new enterprise.

RIGHTS OF COUNSELORS

In addition to the rights set forth in the cases we have just considered and in the codes of ethics of your counseling organizations, here are a few rights of which counselors should be aware.

1. Counselors have the right to reasonable compensation for work performed.

2. Counselors have the right to hold an opinion contrary to that of an employer, agency, college, or client and to have an opportunity to make that opinion known.

3. Counselors have the right to act in accordance with the ethical principles of their profession.

4. Counselors have the right to expect that the counseling relationship will be productive.

5. Counselors have the right to be human, to have personal problems, but not allow those problems to interfere with their ability to do their job.

6. Counselors have the right to expect that their relationship with clients will be productive. "If counselors are unable to maintain such a working

relationship with a client, counselors have the right to terminate the relationship by transferring the client to another counselor" (Martin, 1976, p. 16).

REFERENCES

American Psychological Association. 1987. *Casebook on Ethical Principles of Psychologists,* Washington, D.C.: American Psychological Association, Inc.

American Psychological Association. 1981. "Ethical Principles of Psychologists," *American Psychologist, 36,* 633–38.

Martin, M. E. 1976. *Report from the Study Group on Legal Concerns of the Rehabilitation Counselor,* Menomonie, Wis.: University of Wisconsin-Stout.

5

Codes of Ethics

Mr. Ed Schill, an academic counselor in the Office of Academic Advisement, checks his morning appointment calendar. He sees his first appointment is Ann Andrews, an undergraduate English major. Ann is officially an advisee of his colleague, Ms. Connie Parker. Mr. Schill retrieves Ann's file and notices that Ann was in just last week to plan next semester's class schedule with Ms. Parker.

Ann proceeds to tell Mr. Schill of a conversation she had yesterday with the chairman of her department during which she shows him a copy of her class schedule for the next semester. Upon seeing it, he gets very angry and exclaims, "This is a typical mistake that those advisors would make—you can't register for this seminar, you haven't taken any of the prerequisites!" Ann is very upset that she has registered incorrectly and that the early registration dates have passed so that she may be closed out of several courses. When Mr. Schill asks why she did not bring this to the attention of Ms. Parker, Ann replies, "I called, but she said she was too busy this week to see me again." Ann is practically in tears with frustration. Mr. Schill assures her that it is not too late to remedy the situation; he will personally take care of correcting her registration and apologize to her department chair. Inside, Mr. Schill is seething; this is the fifth time in the past month that he has had to correct one of Ms. Parker's mistakes.

After Mr. Schill finishes his next appointment, he confronts Ms. Parker in her office. He sees that she is on the telephone. Ms. Parker's secretary, Ms. Hammer, indicates that it is a personal call and that it has been a long one. Mr. Schill checks Ms. Parker's appointment calendar and notices that she had an appointment with a student thirty minutes ago. Inquiring after the student, Ms. Hammer tells Mr. Schill that the student just left. "He said that if he waited any longer he would miss his class."

That afternoon Ms. Parker knocks on Mr. Schill's door. "I understand that you wanted to see me," she says. Mr. Schill confronts Ms. Parker with the Ann Andrews situation and states, "I'm concerned and angry that I've had to cover for you several times in the past month."

Ms. Parker responds somewhat defensively: "I'm sorry, Mr. Schill, it was a stupid mistake, but it could have happened to anyone—you know how difficult it is to keep track of all those course numbers."

Mr. Schill: "I understand, but it's more than this one situation. You have been distracted for several weeks and I'm getting tired of covering for you."

Ms. Parker: "Mr. Schill, you know I've been having problems at home; it's just been very difficult lately. I do appreciate your help, and besides, I've covered for you in the past. I just need a little more time."

Mr. Schill is torn between feelings of anger and sympathy toward Ms. Parker and her troubles. He recalls the time last year when his daughter was very sick and it was hard for him to keep his mind on his work.

Two weeks later Mr. Schill hears a commotion outside his office. A student is shouting at Ms. Parker's secretary, "What do you have to do to get an appointment around here? I've been calling every day for a week and Ms. Parker is never available!" The student storms out. Mr. Schill checks with Ms. Hammer and sees that Ms. Parker has no students scheduled for that afternoon. Inquiring as to why Ms. Parker could not see this student, Ms. Hammer replies, "Ms. Parker told me not to schedule any appointments for this afternoon; she had some errands to run."

How should Mr. Schill proceed? One approach might be to look to the ethical standards of his profession to see if Ms. Parker's behavior violated any of the duties and obligations set forth in those ethical standards. But first, Mr. Schill may want to review the standards to determine what his duties and obligations are.

Standard A.2. of the *Ethical Standards of the American Personnel and Guidance Association* governs the behavior of professionals. It states:

A.2. The member has a responsibility both to the individual who is served and to the institution within which the service is performed to maintain high standards of professional conduct. The member strives to maintain the highest levels of professional services offered to the individuals to be served. The member also strives to assist the agency, organization, or institution in providing the highest caliber of professional services. The acceptance of employment in an institution implies that the member is in agreement with the general policies and principles of the institution. Therefore the professional activities of the member are also in accord with the objectives of the institution. If, despite concerted efforts, the member cannot reach agreement with the employer as to acceptable standards of conduct that allow for changes in institutional policy conducive to the positive growth and development of clients, then terminating the affiliation should be seriously considered. (APGA, 1982, p. 9)

The next section, A.3., speaks to Mr. Schill's obligation when he becomes aware that a member of the profession is not performing to his or her ethical responsibilities as set forth in the Standards. This section states:

A.3. Ethical behavior among professional associates, both members and nonmembers, must be expected at all times. When information is possessed that raises doubt as to the ethical behavior of professional colleagues, whether Association members or not, the member must take action to attempt to rectify such a condition. Such action shall use the institution's channels first and then use procedures established by the State Branch, Division, or Association. (APGA, 1982, p. 9)

Mr. Schill reviews the standards in order to determine whether Ms. Parker has violated them and in the process becomes aware of his own ethical responsibility under those standards. But the standards do not speak any further to the point. It is now up to Mr. Schill to decide how he wishes to proceed in order to satisfy his obligation set forth in Section A.3.

He may choose one or more of the following courses of action. He may point out to Ms. Parker that, as a professional, her conduct is governed by the standard of the profession as enumerated in A.2. He may remind her of her obligations as a professional, including the obligation to uphold the standards of her profession. He may choose to bring those professional standards to the attention of the student. He could tell the student that Ms. Parker is required to uphold the standards of the profession and any breach thereof may be a cause for review under the procedures outlined by the American Personnel and Guidance Association. Finally, Mr. Schill might choose to take direct action by filing a complaint with the American Personnel and Guidance Association and request an investigation and a hearing into the matter. If he felt the offense required a less drastic remedy, he might bring the matter to the attention of Ms. Parker's superior, with the assumption that the supervisor is responsible for ensuring that Ms. Parker's behavior conforms to the standards of the profession.

As discussed in chapter 1, one necessary condition for the definition of a profession is that its members have a code of conduct, a set of ethical standards. (Examples of some professional codes of ethics can be found in the Appendix.)

What role do the codes of ethics play?

For one thing, these codes serve as the rules and regulations of the profession. They are the canons of a profession through which the conduct of its members is governed. Members enforce the code and, in turn, their behavior is answerable to its provisions. This type of internal regulation of a profession is termed "self-policing." Society expects and relies upon professional organizations to police the behavior of its members, including setting minimum standards of competence and weeding out incompetent practitioners.

Insofar as the profession adequately governs the conduct of its members, it deflects attempts by federal and state governments to impose regulations on the members of the profession. Professionals need to demonstrate to the "public" that they can adequately address abuses by their own members through the enforcement of the profession's rules and regulations. Whenever organizations fail in these areas, government pressure increases for federal and/or state agencies to step in.

Recent examples of government intervention can be found at the federal level. The Family Educational Rights and Privacy Act makes available psychological information to students or parents indirectly through their surrogates. Congress adopted this law in part because of numerous complaints from parents and students that professionals in the education field were not sharing information with them which they believed they had a right to see. When the information was in dispute, students and/or parents had no recourse to challenge its accuracy. At the same time, information was released to others whom the parents and students did not believe had an appropriate right to see it.

It should be noted that John Ladd presented a very thoughtful paper to the American Association for the Advancement of Science (AAAS) workshop on professional ethics entitled "The Quest for a Code of Professional Ethics: An Intellectual and Moral Confusion" (November

1979), in which he suggests that when codes of ethics become "disciplinary" codes or "penal" codes, they are no longer codes of ethics but codes of laws. (In fact, he questions the philosophical appropriateness of calling anything a code of ethics.) He notes that when codes of ethics become primarily disciplinary, their purpose is to punish those members of the profession who act unethically toward other members of the same profession: "such as stealing a client away from a colleague, for making disparaging remarks about a colleague in public, or for departing from some other sort of norm of the profession."

Codes of ethics serve a number of other functions for members of the profession. As mentioned earlier, these codes are a necessary condition for the existence of a profession in the proper sense of the term. Besides educational requirements and licensure, we find that all professions subscribe to some written set of standards. Codes of ethics have the effect of telling the general public what they can expect from members of the profession.

Codes of ethics outline minimal standards of acceptable behavior. Whenever the professional's conduct falls below these standards and clients are subsequently hurt, the standards become part of the basis for determining the appropriateness of the malpractice suit. Judges and juries weigh the counselor's conduct against the standards of the profession as set forth in testimony by colleagues and in written documents, including codes of ethics. Where the conduct fails to measure up to the standard, a counselor may find himself culpable for his actions.

Codes of ethics serve as omnipresent reminders of how much the profession of counseling values the ethical behavior of its members. In this sense, such codes can be viewed as sources of inspiration. The codes remind counselors that, in any given situation, they have certain moral obligations, that they should be sensitive to the ethical consequences of their actions, that they should know their own value system, and should act so as to promote good and minimize harm. We are reminded of the elements of the code but, more importantly, it inspires us to act ethically in the conduct of our daily affairs, both as professionals and as citizens.

For whom is the code of ethics written? Who is the audience? Thus far, the focus has been on code of ethics as directed primarily to the professional. We have seen that codes of ethics are the canons of the counselor's profession. They govern the behavior of the professional. They inspire ethical conduct and serve as the standard against which professional conduct is measured. Moreover, they serve as a guide or reference for the counselor who has a question about how to proceed after confronting a problematic situation. Ladd (1979) argues that codes of ethics serve to control the behavior of members or professions. He cites as evidence the fact that, "in the original code of the Royal College of Physicians, members who failed to attend the funeral of a colleague were subject to a fine!" (p. 157). Along the same line, codes of ethics may protect professionals from having their clients stolen by other members.

Another audience is the general public. Codes of ethics are designed to say to the general public, "You come to us as clients and these are the standards that we will follow in the course of your care." For example, Principle 6 of the *Ethical Principles of Psychologists* addresses the welfare of the consumer. It states in part: "Psychologists respect the integrity and protect the welfare of the people in groups with whom they work. When conflicts of interest arise between clients and psychologists' employing institutions, psychologists clarify the nature and direction of their loyalties and responsibilities and keep all parties informed of their commitments. Psychologists fully inform consumers as to the purpose and nature of an evaluation, treatment, educational or training procedure, and they freely acknowledge that clients, students, or participants in research have freedom of choice in respect to participation" (APA, 1981, p. 636). Under the same general principle, section 6E states: "Psychologists terminate a clinical or consulting relationship when it is reasonably clear that the consumer is not benefiting from it. They offer to help the consumer locate alternative sources of assistance" (APA, 1981, p. 636).

Ethical standards reassure the public of the quality of the care to be received from the members of the profession. Principle 6A of the *Ethical Principles of Psychologists* states: "Psychologists are continually cognizant of their own needs and of their potentially influential position vis-à-vis persons such as clients, students, and subordinates. They avoid exploiting the trust and dependency of such persons. Psychologists make every effort to avoid dual relationships that could impair their professional judgment or increase the risk of client exploitation. Examples of such dual relationships include, but are not limited to, research with and treatment of employees, students, supervisees, close friends, or relatives. Sexual intimacies with clients are unethical" (APA, 1981, p. 636).

ENFORCING CODES OF CONDUCT

Since a primary role of codes of conduct is to function as a minimum set of rules and regulations, a number of the helping professions, as well as other groups, have adopted formal rules of procedure for adjudicating charges of unethical conduct against members of their association. When a member is charged, these procedures provide an opportunity for a hearing, set forth the member's rights, and, if the member is found guilty, outline sanctions that may be imposed. Let's look at how this works.

The American Psychological Association established an ethics committee and procedures for adjudicating complaints lodged against any of its members alleging some violation of the *Ethical Principles of Psychologists* (ECAPA, 1985). "The Committee has the power to investigate allegations of unethical scientific and professional conduct that may be harmful to the public or to colleagues, or that is otherwise contrary to or destructive of the objectives of the Association" (ECAPA, 1985, p. 685). Complaints of violating the association's ethical principles may be filed against any member, including those who are applying for membership. Anyone—client, licensing board, state or federal agency—may file a complaint that a psychologist has violated the profession's ethical standards. The ethics committee has a special obligation to review cases when a member of the association has been convicted of a felony or when a member has "been expelled or suspended for unethical conduct from an affiliated state or regional association, or has had a license or certificate revoked on ethical grounds by the State Board of Examiners . . ." (ECAPA, 1985, p. 688).

If a member is found guilty of violating the code of ethics, possible sanctions might include expulsion and permitted resignation. These sanctions can only be implemented by the board of directors. The committee itself can "place the member on probation or may reprimand or censure the member. It may also request that the member cease the challenged conduct, accept supervision, or seek rehabilitative or educational training or psychotherapy" (ECAPA, 1985, p. 686). The committee may also recommend that the board delay accepting the resignation of a member pending resolution of a state proceeding against that member or that the board of directors void the membership of an individual (if the membership is obtained on a fraudulent or false basis) or deny the application or form that was supplied for readmission. While the sanctions cited go to the question of a member's status in the American Psychological Association, perhaps the most significant sanction, from a client's perspective, is when the member has been placed on probation, suspended, or there has been a stipulated resignation. The committee may forward this information to the appropriate licensing boards and notify affiliated associations or organizations of its action.

In serious cases that have resulted in a member's probation, suspension, or stipulated resignation, the committee may communicate these actions to: (a) members, (b) committees and divisions of the association, (c) affiliated state and regional associations, (d) the American Board of Professional Psychology (ABPP) and state licensing and certification boards, (e) legal counsel of the association, (f) staff of the association central office designated by the executive officer to assist the committee in its work, (g) the American Association of State Psychology Boards (AASPB), (h) the Counsel for the National Register of Health Service Providers in Psychology (CNRHSPP) and other individuals or organizations as the committee may deem necessary to maintain the highest level of ethical behavior by the member or to protect the public. In addition, the committee may disclose to any of the above organizations or individuals that an individual is under ethical investigation in cases deemed to be serious threats to the public welfare (as determined by two-thirds vote of the committee at a regularly scheduled meeting) and only when to do so before final adjudication appears necessary to protect the public. (ECAPA, 1985, p. 687)

The procedure itself works as follows. The committee chairman and the administrative officer (a staff member of the association so designated as the administrative officer for ethics by the executive officer of the association) review each complaint. They then determine if there is probable cause and in the process they may ask for additional information or refer it for committee action. If both the chairman and the executive officer determine that the behavior did not constitute a violation of the code, the complaint may be dismissed. If the case is accepted, it is then referred to the committee.

The committee has the authority to resolve a complaint by issuing a cease and desist order, a reprimand, censure, requiring the complainant receive supervision, undergo rehabilitation, additional education, training or psychotherapy, be placed on probation, or refer the matter to the appropriate state association or board of examiners. The committee may also recommend stipulated "resignation." That is, if the committee finds that the complainee has committed a serious violation of the ethical principles, in lieu of a formal charge, the committee may recommend to the board of directors that the complainee be permitted to resign and reapply for membership in the association under a stipulated condition. "Should the complainee accept the determination, the case continues to be open until the completion of the stipulated time period and the successful discharge of the stipulated behavior at which time the complainee may reapply for membership and the new application materials and the case file shall be reviewed for readmission by the committee" (ECAPA, 1985, p. 692).

When the committee believes that there has been a serious violation of the ethical principles, it may recommend that formal action be taken by the board of directors by filing with it a formal charge stating that the committee concluded that there is probable cause to believe that the member has violated one or more of the ethical principles of the association. When formal action is taken, the complainee is sent a formal charge which includes "a description of the nature of the complaint, the conduct in question, and citation to the specific section(s) of the *Ethical Principles* that the complainee is alleged to have violated" (ECAPA, 1985, p. 692). Also included is the sanction recommended by the committee. The complainee has a right to request a formal hearing in which time the hearing committee is established to adjudicate the formal charges. The right of the complainee includes "the right to have counsel at the complainee's expense, to present witnesses and documents, and cross-examine witnesses offered by the Ethics Committee. The complainee must provide the Ethics Committee and the Hearing Committee with all documents and names of witnesses and be offered at least fifteen days prior to hearing" (ECAPA, p. 93).

There are no formal rules of evidence and the ethics committee has the burden of proving the charges by a preponderance of the evidence. The hearing committee has thirty days from the date of the conclusion of the hearings to make a decision. The hearing committee, by simple majority, may determine that the complainee is not guilty of the charges, should be allowed to resign from the association, be dropped by the organization, or be formally sanctioned. The choices of the board include expulsion from the association and permitted resignation under stipulated conditions.

LIMITATIONS OF ETHICS CODES

There are a number of shortcomings with codes of ethics. First, such codes do not work particularly well as reference guides professionals can consult on how to act when confronted with a specific problematic situation. For example, take the case of a principal who asks of a school counselor to see the record of a student counselee. The counselor may believe that the principal's request is unjustified. Can the counselor turn to the *Ethical Standards of the American Personnel and Guidance Association* and quote the appropriate section justifying his decision not to share the contents of a student's record?

Section B.5. states: "Records of the counseling relationship, including interview notes, test data, correspondence, tape recordings and other documents, are to be considered professional information for use in counseling and should not be considered a part of the records of the institution or agency in which the counselor is employed unless specified by state statute or regulation. Revelation to others of counseling material must occur only upon the express consent of the client" (APGA, 1982, p. 10).

Now, do we really expect that a school counselor can say to his principal, "I can only show you the record if I get the expressed consent of the parent of the child about whom you are inquiring?" While the regulation sounds fine, the reality of the situation is that it offers no assistance in determining what the counselor should do in this particular situation. Codes of ethics are drafted and adopted as very broad, general guidelines, covering multiple situations and, in general, they have lost the ability to serve as specific answers to a counselor's question regarding any particular situation.

Second, sections of the code may conflict with other codes, laws, and judicial decisions. Taking another example from the *Ethical Standards of the American Personnel and Guidance Association,* Section B.4., under Counseling Relationship: "When the client's condition indicates that there is a clear and imminent danger to the client or others, the member must take reasonable personal action or inform responsible authorities. Consultation with other professionals must be used where possible. The assumption of responsibility for the client's behavior must be taken only after careful deliberation. The client must be involved in the resumption of responsibility as quickly as possible" (APGA, 1982, p. 10).

How does this section measure up to the responsibility of the counselor when dealing with "clear and imminent danger to the client or others" as interpreted by the Supreme Court of California? In the case of *Tarasoff* v. *Regents of the University of California* (529, P2d 553, 1974), the courts made clear that the professional's obligation was not only to inform the university police but, where harm was threatened, the counselor was under an obligation to inform others, including the intended victim. In the Tarasoff decision the court stated: "We conclude that a doctor or a psychotherapist treating a mentally ill patient, just as a doctor treating physical illness, bears a duty to use reasonable care to give the threatened person such warnings as are essential to avert foreseeable danger arising from his patient's condition or treatment" (*Tarasoff,* p. 559).

Therefore, it would appear, given this ruling, that the duty of the counselor to warn is much greater than that set forth in the *Ethical Standards of the American Personnel and Guidance Association.* This is not surprising because, in most cases, codes of ethics of professional organizations are reactive rather than proactive. After a sufficient body of ethical conduct develops that runs counter to that contained within the regulations, the professional organization establishes a task force or some other vehicle to draft amendments to the regulations.

It may even happen that an entirely new code is adopted. For example, during the consumer-conscious period of the 1970s, the American Psychological Association revised its code no fewer than three times and, in addition, it adopted five separate codes of ethics for the specific subsets of the APA *(Guidelines for Psychologists Conducting Growth Groups,* 1973; *Standards for Educational and Psychological Tests,* 1977; *Guidelines for Therapy with Women,* 1978; *APA Guide to Research Support,* 1981; *Ethical Principles in the Conduct of Research with Human Participants,* 1983).

What is it to which the professional organizations are reacting? The change is a response to judicial decisions like Tarasoff or acts of the legislature like New York State's Truth in Testing law. Again it is not surprising but natural to expect that there would be a lag between the ethical standards set forth by professional organizations and the actual behavior of professionals as governed by judicial decision and legislative action. Therefore, because changes in professional practices are guided by judicial decision and legislative action, it may not even be possible to keep codes of conduct current by revising them every year rather than every four or five years, which has generally been the practice (although it should be noted that it is now six years since the last major revision of the code of ethics of a professional counseling organization).

Third, many topics exist on which the codes of ethics are silent, therefore giving the counselor no guidance on how to act when confronted with such a situation. An example of silence by all current codes of ethics of professional organizations has to do with AIDS. Should school counselors notify principals when it is learned that a pupil has AIDS? Does an AIDS carrier represent a clear and present danger to others so as to justify a breach of confidentiality? Are professionals obligated to inform a sexual partner, parents, authorities?

Finally, even when the codes do give answers to questions surrounding a given situation, the codes do not explain how to choose one action over another. What rationale is to be given for acting one way rather than another? In a sense, the ethics codes really do not educate counselors on why they ought to act ethically and why one particular course of action is more appropriate than another. The codes fail to make us more ethical by educating us as to what behavior is ethical and why. Counselors use other devices in order to understand their ethical responsibility, to become ethically sensitive, and to develop a personal methodology for resolving ethical conflicts confronted in the course of professional practice. One part of the methodology will be to review the codes of conduct of the professions. Given the shortcomings of the codes, they can never be more than part of the process in guiding the ethical conduct of counselors.

REFERENCES

American Personnel and Guidance Association, *Ethical Standards* (new ed.). 1982. Falls Church, Va.: American Personnel and Guidance Association.

American Psychological Association (APA). 1981. "Ethical Principles of Psychologists," *American Psychologist* **36** (6), 633.

American Psychological Association. 1973. *Ethical Principles in the Conduct of Research with Human Participants,* Washington, D.C.: American Psychological Association.

American Psychological Association. 1973. "Guidelines for Psychologists Conducting Growth Groups," *American Psychologist* **28** (10), 933.

American Psychological Association. 1977. *Standards for Educational and Psychological Tests,* Washington, D.C.: American Psychological Association.

American Psychological Association. 1978. "Guidelines for Therapy with Women," *American Psychologist* **30,** 1122.

American Psychological Association. 1981. *APA Guide to Research Support,* Washington, D.C.: American Psychological Association.

Ethics Committee of the American Psychological Association (ECAPA). 1985. "Rules and Procedures," *American Psychologist* **40** (6), 685.

Ladd, J. 1979. "The Quest for a Code of Professional Ethics: An Intellectual and Moral Confusion," *Proceedings of AAAS Workshop on Professional Ethics,* 154–59.

Tarasoff v. *Regents of the University of California.* 1974. 529, P2nd 553.

6

Confidentiality

"A fourteen-year-old boy with an extremely high IQ reveals in confidence that he hates his father but loves his mother and will stick by her and protect her. He says he is trying to get his parents to separate by playing tricks on his father. He tells how he places an earring in the car, blonde hairs on his father's coat, and slight traces of lipstick on his father's shirt. His mother, he says, is getting terribly suspicious, and she and his father quarrel over it frequently" (Tenneyson and Strom, 1986, p. 298). As a counselor, what information can you share with the mother and/or father without breaching confidentiality? Are you protected by confidentiality, or privilege, or both? What difference, if any, exists between the two? What should you do if you come to believe that the boy might physically harm his father? Are there any special exemptions here regarding confidentiality because the boy is a minor?

The basic thesis of confidentiality is that both the client and the counselor share ". . . in common a goal of protecting the confidentiality (or secrecy) of communication between persons in a particular relationship where candor and honesty are essential in establishing and maintaining that relationship and where disclosure might destroy it" (Burke, 1985, p. 17). Van Hoose and Kottler (1987) have suggested that the following four criteria be present before communication is considered confidential:

1. The communications must originate with the understanding that they will not be disclosed.

2. Confidentiality must be essential to the maintenance of the relationship.

3. The community must accept the need for confidentiality in the relationship.

4. Injury inflicted on the relationship as the result of disclosure or communication must be greater than the benefit gained from proper disposal of litigation" (Van Hoose & Kottler, p. 50).

Confidentiality is an ethical relationship between the professional and the client. In this relationship both parties promise not to reveal to a third party communication that arises in their counseling sessions. However, the obligation of confidentiality ceases when both parties agree that the information can be shared. In a sense, they agree to "break the moral contract" to keep the communication confidential. For example, in the above case, the counselor might get the boy to agree to tell his mother what he has done, or allow the counselor to tell the mother. It should be noted that the "moral contract" of confidentiality continues after the counseling relationship is severed, unless otherwise agreed. This means that the moral imperative not to share the confided information remains viable even after the death of the client.

Because confidentiality is a matter of ethics, the relationship between the client and the counselor, as a matter of civil law, is enforced through the counseling contract. A breach of confidentiality becomes an unethical practice that may violate the ethical standards of the counselor's professional association and the rights of the client. Therefore, it may be actionable in the courts in the form of malpractice, invasion of privacy, or breach of contract.

It is important to note that confidential communication must be released under lawful court order (unless protected by privilege). Thus, information received in confidence can be subpoenaed by a court, and the counselor may be forced to testify and release the information. But, unlike privilege, the counselor may refuse to release the information even if so directed by the client. For example, the counselor may wish to decline a client's request to reveal information received in confidence if the counselor believes that the client is using the counselor for illegitimate purposes or that the release of the information is not in the client's best interest. As we will discuss later, the counselor does not have this right if the confidential information is privileged.

One final and important facet of confidentiality is that it applies only to the communication between counselor and client. Any plans to divulge confidential communication to counseling staff, consultants, and supervisors should be disclosed to the client and prior approval obtained. Access to confidential information by professional and support staff is an agonizing problem and an ongoing source of concern. It is important that a counselor keep support staff access to a minimum and define limits of their legitimate right to know. This problem has become exacerbated because of the movement by agencies to computerize their records.

To recapitulate, a confidential communication is defined as a communication shared between two parties, both of whom agree not to divulge it to a third party. While we would like to think that our promises of complete confidentiality could never be compromised, it is the case that both professional organizations and the courts have recognized limits on confidentiality. These limits will be discussed in greater detail later in this chapter, limits such as the obligation to reveal confidential information when the counselor believes that the client will harm himself or others. However, at this point in our discussion, it is important that we take some time to compare and contrast the concepts of confidentiality and privilege.

CONFIDENTIALITY VERSUS PRIVILEGE

Within the generic notion of confidentiality exists a small subset of communications that society agrees are so important as to warrant the further protection of being considered privileged. All privileged communications are confidential, but not all confidential communications are privileged. This can be explained in part because confidentiality is a broad ethical concept, while privilege is a more restricted legal concept. Confidentiality is a contract between two parties, the counselor and the client, whereby each agrees not to share the information he receives with a third party. Privilege, as defined in legal statute, prohibits the person with privilege from sharing information that person receives with *anyone* else. Privilege does not apply to the client but only to the counselor. Confidentiality is breached if either party discusses or releases the information he received in confidence. Privilege is breached when the counselor, without the permission of the client, shares the information with a third party.

Confidentiality is a bilateral relation; both parties must agree to dissolve the contract, thereby releasing each other from their mutual obligations not to reveal anything that takes place in the counseling relationship. Privilege, on the other hand, is unilateral; clients are free to share the information with anyone, anywhere, and at any time. However, this in no way changes the nature of the privileged information that the cunselor is still obligated not to discuss.

Privilege is not as absolute as this statement may imply. As we will see in a moment, there are limits. For example, there are legal precedents that give some freedom to the counselor to release information when it appears that the client has misused it. However, once a client authorizes a counselor to release privileged communication, the counselor must comply and has no right to continue to withhold the information. Except where indicated, privileged communication can even be exempt from lawful court order. This is because society views such communication as sacred; without the client's permission, counseling professionals are forbidden to reveal privileged information, even when testifying in a court. Examples can be seen in other professions: a physician is not allowed to reveal information disclosed while treating a patient, a priest is not permitted to disclose a confession, or a lawyer is protected from testifying against his client.

The results and obligations of privilege may extend beyond the counselor and the client. Essentially, the state statutes on privilege set forth an umbrella of privilege which applies to all the employees of the professional. So not only does the professional have privilege, but privilege may also apply to his or her assistants, secretaries, and so on. For example, it is not possible for a court to learn of communication between a lawyer and his client by subpoenaing the lawyer's legal assistant or secretary.

In summary then, we can identify the following features which compare and contrast the principles of confidentiality and privilege.

Confidentiality	Privilege
Ethical	Legal
Contract	Legislature
Mutual	Professional
Symmetrical	Asymmetrical
Either party can breach	Only professional can breach
Limited	Close to absolute

PRIVILEGE

Many stories report the origin of the concept known as privilege. The most credible version is that privilege was first granted by the king of England to physicians during the plague of the Middle Ages. Prior to that time, individuals afflicted with the plague who sought help from a physician were identified as carriers and driven from their village. This exile hastened the plague's spread from village to village. Consequently, the king of England reasoned that the information that a villager was a plague carrier be kept confidential so that the villager would not flee in fear, thereby containing the spread of the plague. By royal decree, the king prohibited the physician from disclosing the medical conditions of his patient (Denkowski, 1982). Students may draw a parallel between this early social response to contagious disease and the response in the 1980s to AIDS.

In New York State the following individuals are granted privilege in differing degrees: spouse, physician, clergyman, lawyer, licensed clinical psychologist, and certified social worker. Privileged communication is privileged forever, even after the death of one of the parties. Privilege, however, is not absolute: it applies only to past, not future, conduct. The courts have ruled that a person with privilege must report to the authorities that a client plans to commit a crime, even though that information is received in confidence under the cloak of privilege.

Privilege extends to communication between a husband and wife, except in matters of proving or disproving the issue of marriage or adultery (New York Evidence Law, 1988, Sec. 4502). However, even though communication between spouses is privileged in New York State, if it takes place in the presence of a third party, the latter is not protected under the umbrella of privilege. For example, the Supreme court held that when a husband chose to communicate to his wife through a stenographer, even though the communication between the husband and wife was confidential, the stenographer could be called to testify (*Wolfe* v. *United States,* 291, US 7 [1934]). Also, the courts have held that if the husband and wife choose to communicate in the presence of their children, again, while the communication between the husband and wife is confidential, the children do not have privilege, and consequently can be called to testify to reveal the communication (*Wolfe* v. *United States,* 291, US 7 [1934]).

The courts have ruled that not even divorce terminates the privilege for confidential marital communications between a husband and a wife. Some courts have also found that "although marital communications are presumed to be confidential, that presumption may be overcome by proof of facts showing that they were not intended to be private" (*Pereira et al.* v. *US* 74 S.Ct. 3558). One of the ways to demonstrate that marital communications are not presumed to be confidential is to show that they occur in the presence of a third party. Therefore, courts have allowed a wife to be called as a witness to testify in a case involving her husband, ruling that privilege did not apply because "the presence of the third party negates the presumption of privacy" (*Pereira,* p. 361).

Communication between a member of the clergy acting in his or her capacity as a spiritual advisor is confidential unless the person speaking waives the right (NY Evidence Law, 1988, Sec. 4505).

Privileged communication between a patient and physician, dentist, or nurse was enacted under New York State law in 1876. Like privileged communication for the clergy, "unless the patient waives the privilege, a person authorized to practice medicine or dentistry or a registered professional or a licensed practical nurse shall not be allowed to disclose any information which he acquired in attending a patient in a professional capacity and which was necessary to enable him to act in that capacity" (NY Evidence Law, 1988, Sec. 4504).

There are, however, two exceptions to this privilege. First, physicians, dentists, and nurses are required to disclose information when the patient is a minor (under the age of sixteen) and has been a victim of a crime (e.g., violent assault, rape, gunshot wounds, stabbings, etc.). Similarly, there are certain circumstances in which the physician or nurse may be required to disclose information about the mental condition of someone who has died (New York Evidence Law, 1988).

Besides privileged communication between a physician and patient, the notion of privilege with which we are probably most familiar is that between a lawyer and a client. Simply stated, all communication between an attorney and a client pertaining to past acts is considered privileged. At this point it should be noted again that in cases where privilege extends to members of a profession, the privilege is not only for the communication between the patient or client and the professional; the umbrella of privilege also extends to the members of the professional staff, including nurses, secretaries, and assistants. This notion of the umbrella of privilege or the umbrella of confidentiality is an important point that to some degree qualifies the notion that privilege and confidentiality are breached if the information is known to a third party. The exception to this rule, and one recognized in law, is when the third party is a member of the professional staff and is assisting the professional in discharging his duties to the client or patient.

Two other members of the helping professions have privilege under New York State law. They are licensed clinical psychologists and certified social workers. The law extends to psychologists registered under the provisions of New York State law all the rights and privileges provided to attorneys (NY, CPLR, 1987). On the other hand, the state law specifically spells out the terms and conditions of privilege for certified social workers registered under applicable New York State law. It states that a certified social worker

> shall not be required to disclose a communication made by his client to him, or his advice given thereon, in the course of his professional employment, nor shall any clerk, stenographer or other person working for the same employer as the certified social worker or for the certified social worker be allowed to disclose any such communication or advice given thereon; except, 1. that a certified social worker may disclose such information as the client may authorize; 2. that a certified social worker shall not be required to treat as confidential a communication by a client which reveals the contemplation of a crime or harmful act; 3. where the client is a child under the age of 16, and the information acquired by the certified social worker indicates that the client has been a victim or subject of a crime, the certified social worker may be required to testify fully in relation thereto upon any examination, trial or other proceeding in which the commission of such crime is the subject of inquiry; . . . privilege is also waived when the client brings charges of professional misconduct against a certified social worker. . . ." (NY, CPLR, 1987, Section 4508)

Many attempts have been made in recent years to extend prior privilege in New York State to other members of the helping professions. In other states privilege has been successfully extended to school counselors, college student personnel administrators, counselors of substance abusers, and others. Readers should consult the laws of their respective states to determine if the relationship between client and counselor is one of confidentiality or one of confidentiality and privilege.

CONFIDENTIALITY AND MINORS

Special issues arise for the counselor when the client is a minor. Fundamental to any counseling relationship is the trust that develops between clients and counselors. Only when that trust exists will clients be prepared to be forthcoming in the counseling relationship. Fundamental to the notion of trust is the clients' belief that whatever is told to the counselor will not be repeated to others.

This concept of trust is essential for an effective counseling relationship, whether the client be a minor or an adult. Therefore, counselors have the same obligation to protect the information received from either a minor client or a client who is past the age of majority. A review of the codes of ethics among various professional counseling organizations supports this argument. Their sections on confidentiality do not distinguish between confidentiality for adults and minors. In fact, they speak of confidentiality for all clients: "Clinical mental health counselors have a primary obligation to safeguard information about individuals obtained in the course of teaching, practice, or research. Personal information is communicated to others only with the person's written consent or in those circumstances where there is clear and imminent danger to the client, to others, or to society. Disclosures of counseling information are restricted to what is necessary, relevant, and verifiable" (Callis, 1982, p. 175).

It would seem, then, that there ought to be no issue: minor clients are to be treated the same as adult clients. *But children are not adults.* Children are a varied population; minor differences in age can result in major differences in rationality, understanding, and maturity. A year can make a vast difference in a minor's basic reasoning skills. Therefore, the minor, as we will see in the next chapter, is unable to give informed consent. If children cannot give informed consent, it appears that they cannot enter into or execute a contract for counseling services. Thus, minors cannot enter into a counseling relationship. Consequently, it might be argued that any contract for services between a minor client and the professional must be executed between the minor's parent(s) or legal guardian. Therefore, the rights of confidentiality belong to the parent(s)/legal guardian and not to the minor.

This is not to say that confidentiality is existent when counselors deal with minors. Nevertheless, there is good reason for caution because it would appear that a number of legal principles (e.g., the nature of contractual relationships) may collide when addressing the ethics of how counselors ought to treat communications received from minor clients. As an example of caution, the *American College Personnel Association Statement of Ethics and Professional Standards* recommends that "members explicitly inform students of the nature and/or limits of confidentiality in non-counseling, as well as in counseling relationships" (Callis, 1982, p. 166).

Further complicating this issue is the legal-historical view surrounding the parent-child relationship. With few exceptions, all legal rights are vested in the parent. There exists an unwillingness by legislators to step in, except in very limited and rare situations, and to recognize the emancipated right of decision making for children.

The parent-child relationship leads to another concern for counselors when working with minor clients—i.e., malpractice. Because minors may not be able to give informed consent, and society views as strong the rights of parents until the child reaches the age of majority, counselors must necessarily be concerned about their vulnerability to malpractice litigation, especially in those cases where the counselor conforms to the wishes of the child, but conflicts with the wishes of the parent(s). The lack of guidelines by professional organizations speaking directly to the issue of the rights and obligations of counselors when dealing with minors puts the professional in the uncomfortable position of being second-guessed, not only by colleagues but also by members of a jury who have their own perception of the way to deal with children.

Wagner (1981) conducted an excellent survey that highlighted this lack of clarity regarding confidential modes of communication by minors. Wagner reported that her survey showed a significant difference between the elementary school counselors' attitude toward confidentiality and that of their secondary school counterparts. Wagner found that all the respondents to her questionnaire, regardless of the school setting, explained the limits of confidentiality that applied to their clients. "The majority (80%) answered that they consider such factors as age, maturity and problem when defining those limits" (Wagner, 1981, p. 306). Thus, it appears that the older the client, the more likely the counselor is to treat the child as an adult.

This approach was consistent with the respondents' other answers. They were asked how they would respond to a case where the client (a student) requested that they release information obtained in counseling, but without parental consent. Assuming it was in the child's best interest, elementary school counselors were least likely to release the information without first informing the parents, while secondary school counselors were most likely to follow the wishes of their clients (Wagner, 1981).

Similarly, counselors were asked if they would release information to an outside source on the request of the parents even though the child requested that it not be released. "For example, if the counselor perceived there to be 'no harm' or 'no benefit' in such a disclosure, the majority of the counselors (65%) would follow the wishes of the parents . . . . [W]hen the counselor's judgment coincided with that of the client (i.e., not releasing the information was in the best interest of the child), the total group of counselor respondents were about equally distributed on the agree and disagree sides (48% and 43% respectively) . . . . [I]t seems safe to say that when parents request the release of information opposed by their sons or daughters, counselors may react ambivalently" (Wagner, 1981, p. 306).

Wagner also included several items in her questionnaire to test the confidential nature of the client-counselor relationship when the client revealed illegal activity to the counselor. She found that "further differences were noted between groups of counselors when illegal client behavior, such as a felony, was introduced into the counseling relationship. If the client asked that this information be kept confidential, the elementary school counselors were the most likely to inform the parents or authorities of the illegal behavior if the illegal behavior involved drug possession or sales. The secondary school counselors were the least likely to respond in this manner" (Wagner, 1981, p. 308). It is Wagner's recommendation that "when children and youth are clients, they should have control over the release of information that results from their choice to engage in the therapeutic process. Exceptions would result in cases in which they waived the right by free choice, in cases of documented child abuse, or in cases of threat to self or society. The latter would include suicide attempts or intent to commit some crime in the future" (Wagner, 1981, p. 310).

Wagner (1981) found that "informal discussion of case material with colleagues not directly involved with the client was considered by 80% of the respondents to be a violation of the child's right to confidentiality. There was no significant difference between the three counselor groups (elementary school counselors, middle and junior high school counselors, and secondary school counselors). Although consensus seems evident in belief, practice falls short in this professionally-expected behavior. Again, there was no significant difference by counselor level, but 24% of the counselors reported 'sometimes' or 'frequently' engaging in such informal discussions" (Wagner, 1981, pp. 306–307).

Wagner concluded that of "the informal discussion of case material with individuals not directly involved, some 25% of the sample reporting such behavior seems abusive. It is easy for school counselors to become isolated given their unique roles; it is possible that such isolation encourages violation of counselors' ethical responsibility to their clients. The responsibility for developing a support system with other counselors or helping professionals who must function within similar parameters rests with the individual counselor. Regular sessions to discuss troublesome cases can be of great assistance in reducing isolation, sharing and brainstorming intervention strategies, and promoting one's own continuing education. Furthermore, clients' rights to privacy are respected and protected" (Wagner, 1981, p. 310).

Zingaro (1973) suggests that we conform to the following guidelines to protect the legal and ethical rights of confidentiality when working with children:

1. Whether the topic of confidentiality is discussed or not, all communications between the child-client and counselor are, in fact, confidential (APA, 1981; APGA, 1981). Therefore, the counseling session itself, and not explicit agreements between the counselor and client, determines the validity of confidentiality for the child.

2. Informal discussion of case material, as opposed to a consultation, with persons not directly involved is a breach of confidentiality. Case material may be discussed with another professional when the focus of the discussion is on helping the client. Counselors who feel the need to "vent their feelings" should center the discussion on themselves, keeping the identity of the client private.

3. "Written or oral reports present only data germane to the purposes of the evaluation, and every effort is made to avoid undue invasion of privacy" (APA, 1981, p. 636). If you are asked to report on a child's behavior in the classroom, do not include your opinions of the parents' social standing or the siblings' extracurricular activities.

4. When a client has revealed information that indicates involvement in an activity that is likely to bring harm to himself or herself or to someone else, the counselor should: (*a*) try to persuade the client to discontinue the activity and (*b*) explain the counselor's responsibility to inform appropriate authorities about the "condition" without revealing the client's identity. If steps (*a*) and (*b*) do not deter the client, the counselor is ethically bound to (*c*) "take reasonable personal action or inform responsible authorities" (APGA, 1981, p. 1). The authorities (parents, school, legal) will be determined by the context of the situation and the counselor's judgment of which authority will best serve the needs of the client.

5. If the counselor is subpoenaed to testify in a legal proceeding but does not wish to reveal information and in so doing protect the client's best interests, the counselor may: (*a*) become an agent of the client's attorney (That is, by revealing the child's case, the

counselor may invoke the attorney-client—the counselor in this case—privilege. The attorney must raise the privilege in court for the counselor to be protected by it.) and (*b*) request that the information be received in the judge's chamber rather than in open court. Neither of these options guarantees the counselor's privilege not to reveal information. "Ethical codes do not supersede the law" (Stude & McKelvey, 1979, p. 456).

6. In instances in which the counselor is not sure of actions to be taken, "consultations with other professionals must be used where possible" (APGA, 1981, p. 1). Other professionals include, but are not limited to, members of the pupil personnel team, school administrators, community mental health agencies, the school solicitor, university professors, and various experts in the field (errors of omission or commission may be more expensive than a long-distance phone call).

7. When parents or school personnel request information about the client, the counselor should first consider the client's right to privacy. If, in the counselor's judgment, significant others have a need to know and revealing information would be in the child's best interest, the counselor should respond by telling these adults what they can do or refrain from doing to help the child. In this way the child's communications are still privileged. In the author's experience this suggestion has been well received by parents and teachers. Adults who request information because they are curious or truly interested in their child's welfare seem satisfied with this approach (Zingaro, 1983, p. 265).

CONFIDENTIALITY IN GROUP COUNSELING

As we have seen, fundamental to the counseling relationship is the establishment of trust between client and counselor, as is their mutual belief that what they communicate in the counseling session will not be divulged to anyone else. Nowhere in counseling is this axiom truer than in group counseling. "In the group experience there is an expectation as part of the group's process for all members of the group to share with one another feelings and thoughts about self which they would not usually disclose to others and to volunteer their feelings and thoughts towards others in the group in an open and genuine manner" (Caple, 1976, p. 193).

Yet confidentiality is a very difficult thing in group counseling. The definition of confidentiality—communication between two parties that both agree not to reveal to a third—would appear to make it impossible to have the traditional sense of confidentiality in group work. While an operational definition of confidentiality is possible, the nature of group dynamics militates against the desire to keep confidential the information exchanged within the group process. This was the sense of reality gleaned by Davis when she tested how group leaders and members treated confidentiality in their groups.

Davis (1983) found that group leaders and members valued confidentiality, but were confused about the way confidentiality is discussed and what its limits are within the group setting. Does this confusion mean that participants cannot talk to anyone about what goes on in the group, including family and friends? Even though the American Personnel and Guidance Association (APGA) guidelines clearly state that group leaders shall discuss confidentiality with the group, a number of group leaders surveyed by Wagner were not sure how and when to bring up the subject. The Association of Specialists in Group Work (ASGW) ethical guidelines for group leaders has a similar provison: "Group leaders shall protect members by defining clearly what confidentiality means, why it is important, and the difficulties involved in enforcement" (ASGW, 1980, Sec. A–3).

Given the findings by Davis, how should counselors proceed to best protect the information obtained from clients in group counseling sessions? Davis suggests that the group leader discuss confidentiality during both the screening interview and the first meeting. Additionally, the group leader should discuss confidentiality at other times during group sessions, as appropriate and as the circumstances may warrant. She suggests that during the screening interview the group leader "clearly delineate to whom the leader may talk and what information the leader may share with a group or nongroup member. At the first meeting, the leader should explain the restrictions a leader has regarding group information and ask members if they have any questions about the leader's commitment to confidentiality. By discussing the leader's need to respect confidentiality the members would have a clear idea of what will happen with any member disclosures and not have to speculate on the leader's professional judgment" (Davis, 1983, p. 200). Davis suggests that at this first meeting, the leader's discussion of confidentiality would be enhanced if the members were asked to give examples of the categories of people they would like to share their information with, and why they feel the need to disclose. This discussion allows the leader to initiate a conversation about confidentiality around the specific examples cited by members of the group. Davis further suggests that this meeting include a discussion of possible consequences for violations of confidentiality or trust. Ultimately, the discussion should lead to an agreement by members of the group on the limits of confidentiality.

The ultimate outcome of such a discussion, according to Davis, might be a contractual agreement between the leaders and the members of the group. A contract would not guarantee that all communication within the group will remain confidential. However, it would be a substantial step in the direction of ensuring that the leaders and the members of the group respect the confidential nature of the communications that occur within the group. For example, will the counselor be sharing this information with anyone else? If so, with whom and under what conditions? Will the counselor be sharing the information with a supervisor; with law enforcement (courts, attorneys, or the police); with an intern who might be listening to tapes of the sessions; with a colleague if the counselor feels that the advice of the colleague is needed? Will the client be sharing the information with anyone else? If so, under what circumstances? Will the client be sharing the information with a spouse; a parent; a child; a friend; or with another professional, such as a physician or a teacher? Consequently, all members of the group will understand the circumstances under which information may be shared with others.

These qualifying conditions of the contractual relationship need to be explored and agreed upon by all parties prior to the beginning of counseling. By doing so, the parties will have a very clear understanding of the true nature of confidentiality in the relationship, an opportunity to understand how everyone understands the term, as well as an opportunity to comment on and help define the contract of confidentiality.

The American College Personnel Association has also felt the need to establish ethical guidelines for individuals involved in group work. A task force of the ACPA spent five years developing a comprehensive statement guiding the ethical conduct of professional group facilitators at all levels of activity. The section pertaining to confidentiality reads as follows:

7. Confidentiality. The group facilitator will respect the confidentiality of information generated about individual members within a group.

a. The facilitator will discuss a group he is facilitating or individuals within the group only with persons clearly concerned with the group and then only for professional purposes. . . .

b. Although assurance cannot be provided by the facilitator, group members will be informed of their mutual responsibility to refrain from revealing outside the group the confidences gained in the group.

c. Audio or video tape, or other data collected within the group, may be utilized only by the group members unless all members of the group give their expressed, written permission for its specified use in other circumstances.

d. The use of data generated in a group for classroom teaching or for writing will be done only when the identity of the group and its members is adequately disguised. (Caple, 1976, p. 167)

CONFIDENTIALITY AND AIDS

Many times the confidential nature of communication between counselor and client is reinforced in state law. The counselor is encouraged to consult pertinent state laws to see if there are any specific statutes governing the release of information obtained in the counseling setting. For example, New York State recently considered adopting the Acquired Immune Deficiency Syndrome Testing Confidentiality Bill. This act would prohibit the release of AIDS test results except under very limited circumstances. Included as an exception is the release to "a State or local health official where such disclosure is made by a physician, upon sworn affidavit, that during the process of medical treatment, a patient has demonstrated to the physician, through direct communication, that such patient will not inform an identified spouse or sexual partner of the test results or will not use medically accepted techniques which are believed to prevent transmission during intercourse provided, however, such State or local health officer shall, notwithstanding any inconsistent provision of law to the contrary, be authorized to redisclose such information for the sole purpose of direct notification of such contacts provided further, that the provisions of this paragraph shall not be construed to authorize the disclosure or redisclosure of the index name of the patient. . ." (New York Assembly, Bill 6924-c, 1987–88 Regular Session).

REFERENCES

American Personnel and Guidance Association (APGA). 1981. *Ethical Standards* (rev. ed.), Falls Church, Va.

American Psychological Association (APA). 1981. "Ethical Principles of Psychologists," *American Psychologist* **36** (6), 633.

Association for Specialists in Group Work. "Ethical Guidelines for Group Leaders" (approved on November 11, 1980).

Burke, R. E. 1985. "Privileges and Immunities in American Law," *South Dakota Law Review* **31**, 17.

Callis, R.; Pope, S. K.; and DePauw, M. E. 1982. *Ethical Standards Casebook,* Falls Church, Va.: American Personnel and Guidance Association.

Caple, R. B. 1976. "The Use of Group Procedures in Higher Education: A Position Statement by ACPA," *Journal of College Student Personnel.*

Davis, K. L. 1983. "Is Confidentiality in Group Counseling Realistic?" *The Personnel and Guidance Journal* **59**, 200.

Denkowski, K., and Denkowski, G. 1982. "Client-Counselor Confidentiality: An Update of Rational, Legal Status, and Implications," *The Personnel and Guidance Journal* **60** (6), 371–74.

New York Civil Practiced Law and Rule, New York Assembly Bill 6924-c, 1987–88, Regular Session, McKinney (1988).

New York Evidence Law, McKinney. 1988.

Pereira et al. v. *United States,* 74 8 et. 358 (1953).

Stude, E. W., and McKelvey, J. 1979. "Ethics and the Law: Friend or Foe?" *Personnel and Guidance Journal* **57** (9), 453.

Tenneyson, W. W., and Strom, S. M. 1986. "Beyond Professional Standards: Developing Responsibleness," *Journal of Counseling and Development* **64**, 298.

Van Hoose, W. H., and Kottler, J. A. 1978. *Ethical and Legal Issues in Counseling and Psychotherapy,* San Francisco: Jossey-Bass.

Wagner, C. 1981. "Confidentiality and the School Counselor," *Personnel and Guidance Journal* **59** (5), 305.

Wolfe v. *United States,* 291 US 7 (1934).

Zingaro, J. C. 1983. "Confidentiality: To Tell or Not to Tell," *Elementary School Guidance and Counseling* **17** (4), 261.

7

Working with Children

Working with children can raise some very difficult ethical questions for counselors. For example, what is to be done when a child seeks counseling but the parents refuse to give their consent? How is the obligation of confidentiality regarding information received from a minor client to be balanced with respect for the rights of the parents to obtain information about their child? Is it ever appropriate for a counselor to become an advocate for a young client?

This chapter will look at these and other questions by considering two major areas of the counselor-child relationship: informed consent and participation in decisions regarding the course of treatment.

INFORMED CONSENT

As discussed in chapter 3, the rudimentary elements of informed consent are the ability of the client to make a rational choice when presented with options; an environment where the choice is made free of coercion by the counselor or any other party; access to information, which includes, but is not limited to, a description of what is about to happen, in addition to potential risks and benefits; alternative courses of treatment; and a statement of client rights, including the right to have all questions completely and fully answered before treatment commences, and the right to withdraw consent at any time during the course of treatment.

Grisso and Vierling (1978) argue that when we discuss informed consent for minors, we need to consider three variations of the concept: (1) the minor client has a right to consent to treatment independent of his parents' wishes; (2) the minor client has the right to refuse treatment after his parent has given consent; and (3) the minor client does not have a right to agree to or refuse treatment, but a limited right to participate in the discussion about the form of treatment and all other matters that may arise during the course of treatment.

The first variation is the traditional form of informed consent, which is afforded to all adult clients. The essential elements of informed consent, as discussed in greater detail in chapter 3, are knowledge, understanding, and freedom. The key questions regarding minor clients are: (1) does the minor comprehend the information provided to a degree sufficient to make an informed choice; and (2) even if the child understands the information provided, have the youngster's powers of reasoning developed sufficiently to enable an informed choice? To put it another way, can the child weigh competing alternatives, factor in a number of variables germane to the situation, give those variables different weight in the deliberation, and finally choose one of the options over the others?

Grisso and Vierling (1978) list the following elements as indicative of the maturing of a minor. "Among those that might influence consent decision making are one's attention to the task, ability to delay response in the process of reflecting on the issues, ability to think in a sufficiently differentiated manner (cognitive complexity) to weigh more than one treatment alternative and set of risks simultaneously, ability to abstract or hypothesize as yet nonexistent risks and alternatives, and ability to employ inductive and deductive forms of reasoning (p. 418).

The other element in the discussion of informed consent for minor clients is the requirement that the choice be free. This means that the client has made the choice based upon the merits of the particular situation, without threat or undue influence. "Registering one's consent or dissent in treatment situations is a social act. One is asked to announce to a person of some prestige and authority one's decision regarding a proposed treatment or, perhaps more accurately, is requested to comply with a treatment proposal . . . thus it is meaningful to speak of a person's competence to provide *voluntary* consent to treatment—that is, to provide consent that is not merely an acquiescent or deferent response to authority" (Grisso and Vierling, 1978, p. 421).

Freedom of choice requires challenging authority. For most young clients the authority to be challenged is parental. Melton (1980) found that for a young child this can be a virtually impossible act. "According to the work of Piaget (1932/1965) and Kohlberg (1964, 1969, 1976), young children regard rules as 'sacred and untouchable,' external, and emanating from parental or divine authorities. To the extent to which a child holds such a view of moral absolutism he is not likely to challenge authority and claim rights for himself" (p. 186).

A minor does not have the right to consent to counseling services independent of parental wishes or to refuse counseling services after the parents have given consent, except as we will discuss in the next section. Our society views the parent-child relationship as sacred, since the parent is responsible for the welfare of the child. (Legal historians suggest that these rights of parents arise from the notion that the child was perceived under Anglo-Saxon law to be the property of his father.) The only time this relationship can be abridged is when the parent acts to jeopardize the welfare of the child. Then it is appropriate for the courts to act as *parens patriae*. It is suggested by Young (1963) that the legal rights of parents are to be accorded the same high respect as freedom of religion.

Professional counseling organizations have consistently taken the position that it is unethical for a counselor to engage in a counseling relationship with a minor client without first informing the parent of this fact and receiving the parent's consent.

Take, for example, the following case, which was reviewed by the Committee on Professional Standards under the direction of the Board of Professional Affairs of the American Psychological Association.

A psychologist who specialized in family therapy received a telephone call from an attorney requesting that the psychologist evaluate three children, aged three, five and seven, while they were on a weekend visit to their father's home, because their father was suing for custody. Rather than schedule a weekend appointment with the children and their father, the psychologist suggested that the mother be requested to bring the children in for the evaluation, or else that the attorney seek a court order for psychological evaluations. The psychologist noted that he would like to evaluate all persons involved in the care of the children, including other adults who might be living in the home and sharing in the care of the children.

The mother telephoned the psychologist and agreed to bring the children in for an evaluation and to undergo a psychological evaluation herself, as long as her husband was willing to do so.

During the psychologist's interview of the father, the father told the psychologist that he suspected his children were being abused sexually or exposed to elicit drugs by their mother's boyfriend, who lived in the home. The psychologist telephoned this to the Child Protective Services of his state, in accordance with the state legal requirements, to inform them of a possible child abuse case. He was told that the case was under investigation but that so far the agency had nothing to go on. The psychologist also telephoned the little girls' mother to tell her that he had had to notify Child Protective Services. . . .

The father did not accept the court's decision to permit the mother to retain custody. He claimed that the psychologist had been biased in that the report had not taken into consideration the possibility of child abuse, and was not supposed to be recommending one parent over the other anyway. He brought the case to the Ethics Committee of the state psychological association. In its review, the Ethics Committee found that the psychologist had been responsible and clinically effective in many respects. However, the psychologist had no written request for an evaluation that might document the nature of the understanding of what was to be included in the report. There was no written evidence that the psychologist had notified the Child Protective Services regarding the charge of child abuse. Further, the Ethics Committee judged that the psychologist's report contained a number of conclusions about the adequacy of the mother and inadequacy of the father without supporting material or internal justification for the conclusions based on the psychological tests, observations and interviews. (Committee, 1988, p. 557–58)

The Committee on Professional Standards concluded, among other things, that "the psychologist recognized the illegality of doing psychological evaluations on minor children without the knowledge and permission of the custodial parent and appropriately requested that the custodial parent endorse the request for an evaluation" (Committee, 1988, p. 558).

If the minor client does not have the right to give independent consent or to revoke consent given by a parent, how should the counselor proceed? When working with young clients, it is recommended that the counselor obtain written informed consent from the parents *and* should, if at all possible, obtain written informed consent from the minor client. Let us look at a case where neither was done.

A school psychologist was conducting research into the effectiveness of the sex education offered by elementary schools. To evaluate these programs, she decided it was essential that she interview elementary school children themselves. The psychologist interviewed 30 sixth graders about their knowledge and feelings on a variety of issues related to sexuality without first obtaining written permission from their parents.

Several parents complained to the school administration; one submitted a formal complaint to the Ethics Committee. The psychologist responded to the committee's inquiry that she had taken extreme care in preparing the students to be interviewed. She had spoken more than once in class about her research and why she needed to talk with students, and she had received the oral permission of each student she interviewed. Moreover, she had asked the students to speak ahead of time with their parents so that any of their fears could be allayed by the psychologist in a timely fashion. Receiving no word of any objection from any of the students' parents, she assumed that all were amenable to the interviews. (APA, 1987, p. 75)

The Ethics Committee of the American Psychological Association ruled that the psychologist violated Principle 5.d. of the Ethical Principles of Psychologists by failing to "take sufficient care to protect the best interests of a minor. When dealing with a minor, it is the psychologist's responsibility to contact the parents directly. Written, informed consent from both parents and the child is advisable. The Committee voted to censure the psychologist and require that she take a course in scientific ethics at a local university" (APA, 1987, p. 75).

CHILD ABUSE

Child abuse is a paradigm case wherein the counselor's right to promise confidentiality is constricted by higher-order social values. In the case of child abuse the social value of protecting children from harm outweighs any argument that the counselor's action may benefit the child. The limits of confidentiality in cases of abuse are exemplified in the following example from the *Casebook for Providers of Psychological Services* (1988).

A psychologist in private practice had been seeing a husband and wife as a couple for counseling for several months. At termination, the couple brought in their 15-year-old daughter for counseling—explaining that they were concerned over how withdrawn she seemed to have become in recent months. In the course of counseling with the daughter, the psychologist learned from her that she had been and still was being sexually abused by the father. No hint of abuse had been suspected in the earlier counseling with the girl's parents; the matter had never been discussed.

As the parent of a minor, the mother had maintained contact with the psychologist regarding the daughter's counseling. In conversation with the mother, the psychologist broached the matter of the daughter's abuse. The mother confirmed the father's sexual abuse of the daughter and indicated that the abuse continued. The mother shared that she felt that any discussion with the father of the abuse would likely place the daughter in serious danger, and that she would fear for her own as well as her daughter's safety if the abuse were made known to anyone. The mother asserted that she would consider the therapist's reporting of the abuse to anyone to constitute a breach of professional confidentiality. At the mother's insistence, and in consideration of both the daughter's and the mother's safety, the psychologist decided not to report the abuse to appropriate authorities—despite a law requiring psychologists to report any suspected or known cases of abuse within 24 hours.

The psychologist continued to counsel the daughter, attempting to help the daughter deal with the emotional trauma of the abuse and develop skill at avoiding or escaping from abuse by the father.

Several months after the daughter's termination of counseling with the psychologist, personnel at the daughter's school learned of the ongoing abuse and reported it to the authorities. In the course of the ensuing investigation, it was learned that the daughter had been seen by the psychologist and that she had shared that she was being abused by the father. A case was brought against the psychologist by the state for failing to comply with a state statute that requires reporting of known or suspected instances of child abuse to the appropriate authorities on the basis of concern for the welfare of the daughter and her mother. (APA, 1988, p. 559)

The Committee on Professional Standards found the psychologist guilty of violating the General Standards for Providers of Psychological Services. They reasoned as follows: First, professionals are obligated to know the legal limitations of the client's right to confidentiality and are obligated to inform the client of those limits prior to commencing therapy. Second, the counselors are professionally obligated always to act in accordance with the legal limits of their profession. Third, while the psychologist argued that, by not reporting the child abuse he was protecting his client's rights and acting in his client's best interest, the Committee felt that the fact the the abuse continued after the psychologist was informed of it may very well have negated whatever good the psychologist thought he was doing. Finally, the Committee reasoned that "notification of appropriate social service authorities regarding the daughter's abuse and consultation with personnel regarding the daughter's and mother's safety and well-being would have been both professionally and legally responsible. By not contacting and consulting with the appropriate service agency personnel on behalf of the daughter, the psychologist not only was in violation of the state statute, but also failed to make use of professional and administrative sources that have been provided and are available to protect the best interests of minors" (APA, 1988, p. 560).

THE RIGHT TO TREATMENT

One of the most difficult ethical problems facing counselors is knowing how to respond when a minor client seeks treatment. In the classic words of Justice Cardozo, "every human being of adult years and sound mind has a right to determine what shall be done with his own body." If Justice Cardozo's words are taken literally, they will lead the counselor to conclude that there are no circumstances in which it is appropriate to treat a minor client without first receiving consent from the client's parent or legal guardian. A number of states have moved to clarify Justice Cardozo's comment by according the minor the right to treatment independent of parental consent or knowledge. Some states have allowed minor clients to seek treatment, without parental consent, for medical emergencies, birth control, alcohol and drug abuse, pregnancy, and venereal disease. Also, a number of states allow minors above a certain age to seek medical services without parental consent. Even then there may be specific exclusions, such as abortions. In addition, Alabama, Maryland, Oregon, and California permit minors above a particular age to consent independently to mental health treatment, provided certain conditions are met. Since there are such wide discrepancies between the states, readers are strongly advised to be aware of the laws that govern minors in their states.

The action of the courts and society is based upon the recognition that it is the parent who has the obligation to care for the children. Society maintains that this obligation must be free from outside interference unless the parent's action(s) prove harmful to the child.

In the majority of cases confronted by counselors, the problem is to balance the child's right to seek treatment against the parents' right to decline treatment. Melton (1978) provides us with an excellent example of just such a value conflict:

One such case involved Wanda, a fifteen-year-old Honduran girl who had come to an adolescent clinic in a northeastern city ostensibly to inquire about her boyfriend who attended a therapeutic school there. It soon became obvious that Wanda was seeking help for herself: "I feel I am all mixed up, and I want someone to straighten me out." The clinicians who met Wanda felt that she was subject to a schizophrenic disorder and that she was actively decompensating. She was markedly depressed, and she had expressed many suicidal and homicidal ideations. There was a paranoid quality to much of her ideation, and she perceived the world as filled with "evil spirits" (perhaps a family myth). Wanda initially resisted informing her parents of her visit to the mental health center, but she had no qualms about such disclosure on her second visit. While Wanda's parents permitted home visits, they attributed her behavior to silly American ways and felt no need for mental health intervention. Her beliefs, paranoid by the clinician's standards, were consistent with the family's spiritualism. (Melton, 1978, p. 201)

Melton reported that Wanda stopped visiting the clinic when it became apparent that her parents were opposed to her seeking treatment. This raises a related issue, especially germane to minors, that most are reluctant to seek treatment independently without parental support and family involvement.

Conversely, should minor clients have the right to refuse treatment? Shedev (1976) provides us with a good example illustrating why substantial weight should be given to the parents' judgment in such matters.

An intelligent four-year-old is brought by his parents for psychiatric consultation because he is "afraid of strangers." In his first three years of life, he underwent repeated surgical operations in an effort to correct congenital defects. Following his last operation, the child grew repeatedly nervous; he stopped playing with his peers and became isolated in his house. In view of his chronological immaturity he could hardly give "informed" consent, but, more unfortunately, the trauma he suffered "at the hands of doctors-strangers" made him fearful of others, particularly doctors. He did not want to come for psychiatric consultation. If this bright, young, frightened boy were to make his own decision, it would in all probability seriously impede his cognitive, emotional and social growth. (Shedev, 1976, p. 662)

Just because minor clients do not have the right to give independent consent for treatment does not mean that they do not have a qualified right to participate meaningfully in decisions about their treatment. More and more counselors are recognizing their ethical responsibility to allow minor clients a significant say in what is going to happen in the counseling process. "Especially with regard to the general principle of right of self-determination, we are beginning to take seriously the idea that minors are entitled to have some form of consent or dissent regarding the things that happen to them in the name of assessment, treatment, or other professional activities that have generally been determined unilaterally by adults in the minor's interest" (Grisso & Vierling, 1978, p. 412).

Studies have shown that substantial benefits accrue to minor clients when they are allowed a degree of self-determination in the counseling process. Among the identified benefits are: first, the establishment of a healthier relationship between the counselor and the client because such self-determination creates an atmosphere in which the client is respected as a person. In such a relationship the counselor affords the client what Melton (1981) terms "maximum reasonable autonomy." Studies have shown that where clients participate significantly in the therapeutic process and feel a degree of personal control over what is happening to them, they buy in more fully to the process which, in turn, facilitates change.

For example, Holmes and Erie (1975) found that a preparatory interview in which the expectations for psychotherapy are discussed reduced the incidence of premature termination among children aged six to twelve (reported in Melton, 1981). Participation by the minor client in the planning of the course of counseling may make the client less frightened, apprehensive, and reluctant, and even less hostile. It may facilitate the client being more forthcoming and at ease once the treatment regimen begins. Brehm (1966) found that by allowing minor clients to believe they have control over what is going to happen to them reduces reticence and resistance to treatment (reprinted in Melton, 1981).

Allowing the minor client to have the rights of a full citizen in the counseling process may help assuage the unfavorable attitudes the minor may have toward counseling professionals. For example, Dollinger and Thelen (1978) studied children's perceptions of psychology and found that "children strongly conceive of psychology as a therapeutic enterprise," "many children have a limited conception of what psychologists do," and "one cause for concern is that, although knowledge about psychology increased with age, the more evaluative responses were not more positive with increasing age. Moreover, children who had been to a psychologist, who had participated in research, or who had taken a psychology course did not express significantly more favorable attitudes and attraction toward psychology than their classmates. This finding should concern all of us

who work with children in a professional capacity" (Dollinger & Thelen, 1978, p. 125). These researchers conclude with advice that is appropriate for any member of the counseling profession. "Thus, psychologists
should direct critical attention towards current practices regarding how
they present themselves to children. Clearly, as a profession, there is much
to be done to inform our youth about what psychologists are and do.
Such efforts hopefully would result in more young people having a positive
attitude toward psychology and psychologists" (Dollinger & Thelen, 1978,
p. 126).

Finally, Meichenbaum ([1977] reported in Melton [1981]) found that
the practice of allowing children to participate in the discussions and
planning of the treatment regimen has the effect of buffering any stress
that may be present in the therapeutic techniques. Planning sessions serve
as early warning systems, so a young client can begin to prepare mentally
for any perceived stress that may arise in the therapeutic regime. These
sessions also provide an opportunity for dialogue between the counselor
and the minor client, an interaction in which questions raised by the minor
client can be fully addressed, erroneous preconceived notions corrected,
and rapport developed. Melton (1981) reports on the study conducted by
Lewis, Lewis, Lorrimer, and Palmer, (1977) in which elementary school
children were given essentially unlimited access to the school nurse. "Users
of the system showed decreased sense of vulnerability in self-perceived
severity of problems as well as increased belief in the value of self-cure"
(p. 251).

GUIDELINES FOR WORKING WITH MINOR CHILDREN

The following advice should be carefully considered and questions answered
before accepting a minor client without parental consent.

1. Consult legal counsel for advice on pertinent state law on the rights
   of minors regarding consent to therapy (Melton, 1981).

2. Don't be afraid to ask colleagues what they would do in a specific
   situation.

3. Know and follow the applicable rules of your professional organization
   with respect to counseling minors, e.g., the APA's *Ethical Principles
   of Psychologists,* Principle 5.d., which states: "When working with minors
   or other persons who are unable to give voluntary, informed consent,

psychologists take special care to protect these persons' best interests" (APA, 1981).

4. Is your client a "mature minor"?*

5. Is your client an "emancipated minor"?†

6. If there is a risk to the client, how serious is it and what would be the likely consequences if treatment is denied?

7. What is the likelihood of your client's parents denying consent or your client refusing to seek parental permission?

8. Would your client decline to seek help if parental consent were denied?

9. How complex is the proposed treatment and what are its potential risks? (Melton, 1981)

REFERENCES

American Psychological Association. 1981. "Ethical Principles of Psychologists," *American Psychologist* 36 (6), 631.

American Psychological Association. 1987. *Casebook on Ethical Principles of Psychologists,* Washington, D.C.: American Psychological Association, Inc.

Committee on Professional Standards. 1988. "Casebook for Providers of Psychological Services," *American Psychologist* 43 (7), 557.

Dollinger, S. J., and Thelen, M. H. February 1978. "Children's Perceptions of Psychology," *Professional Psychology* 9 (1), 117.

Grisso, T., and Vierling, L. August 1978. "Minors Consent to Treatment: A Developmental Perspective," *Professional Psychology* 9 (3), 412.

Kohlberg, L. 1964. "Development of Moral Character and Moral Ideology." In M. L. Hoffman and L. W. Hoffman (eds.), *Review of Child Development Research,* vol. 1, New York: Russell Sage Foundation.

---

*"Mature minor" is a court-determined status ascribing adulthood to a minor based on cognitive, behavioral, and developmental criteria.

†Emancipated minor" is a court-determined status whereby an individual (generally sixteen years of age) is determined to be responsible for his own welfare. Emancipation is determined by maintenance of a separate residence, marriage, ability to be self-supporting, and so forth.

Kohlberg, L. 1969. "Stage and Sequence: The Cognitive-Development Approach to Socialization." In D. A. Goslin (ed.)., *Handbook of Socialization Theory and Research,* New York: Rand McNally.

———. 1976. "Moral Stages and Socialization: The Cognitive-Development Approach." In T. Lickona (ed.), *Moral Development and Behavior: Theory, Research, and Social Issues,* New York: Holt, Rinehart & Winston.

Melton, G. Fall 1980. "Children's Concepts of Their Rights," *Journal of Clinical Child Psychology* **9,** 186.

———. 1978. "Children's Right to Treatment," *Journal of Clinical Psychology* **7** (Fall), 200.

———. 1981. "Children's Participation in Treatment and Planning: Psychological and Legal Issues," *Professional Psychology* **12** (2), 246.

Shedev, H. S. 1976. "Patients' Rights or Patient Neglect: The Impact of the Patients' Rights Movement on Delivery Systems," *American Journal of Orthopsychiatry* **46** (4), 660.

Young, S. G. 1963. "Parent and Child: Compulsory Medical Care Over Objections of Parents," *West Virginia Law Review* **65,** 184–87.

8

Sexual Relations with Clients

The ethical principles of nearly every professional counseling organization state that it is unethical for counselors to engage in sexual relations with their clients. This prohibition of sexual intimacy with clients is not a recent phenomenon. The Oath of Hippocrates states: "Whatever houses I may visit, I will come for the benefit of the sick, remaining free of all intentional injustice, of all mischief and in particular of sexual relations with both female and male persons, be they free or slaves" (Etziony, 1973, p. 14). Yet each new study on this topic reveals a sizeable number of counselors engaging in such sexual relations. This chapter will focus on why such liaisons continue, the rationale behind the ethical policy prohibiting them, and what guidelines can be developed to help ensure that the counselor's behavior meets the highest ethical standards of the profession.

Principle 6.a. of the *Ethical Standards of Psychologists* states that "psychologists are continually cognizant of their own needs and of their potentially influential position vis-à-vis persons such as clients, students, and subordinates. They avoid exploiting the trust and dependency of such persons. Psychologists make every effort to avoid dual relationships which could impair their professional judgment or increase the risk of exploitation. Examples of such dual relationships include, but are not limited to, research with or treatment of employees, students, supervisees, close friends, or relatives. Sexual intimacies with clients are unethical" (APA, 1981,

101

p. 636). Similar prohibitions against sexual intimacy with clients can be found in most all codes that deal with the behavior of counselors. Nevertheless, in a July 1988 report in the *American Psychologist,* the Ethics Committee of the American Psychological Association (ECAPA) found that "over the past five years almost one quarter (23%) of the violations involved Principle 6.a. (dual relationships including sexual intimacies with clients)" (ECAPA, 1988, p. 565).

In the five-year period from 1982 to 1987, malpractice charges involving sexual intimacy accounted for about 45 percent of the over $15 million paid out by APA's Professional Liability coverage provider (ECAPA, 1988, p. 567). The largest award totaled $2.3 million. As if that were not enough, two states moved to make consensual sexual relations with a client illegal. This illegality may even extend to former patients as well. Violations are considered a felony, with prison terms reaching ten years and maximum fines of $20,000 (ESAPA, 1988, p. 567).

Leaders of numerous counseling professions have spoken out vociferously against sexual intimacies with clients. In 1985 a former president of the American Psychological Association characterized sexual intimacies by American Psychological Association members as "a national disgrace" for the entire profession (ECAPA, 1988).

In spite of all these condemnations, Kenneth S. Pope, Chairman of the American Psychological Association's Ethics Committee, reported in August 1988 that his panel's latest survey of "distinguished psychologists from across the country" found eighty-two incidents of "sexual intimacies between therapists and minor patients." From the ninety who replied to the survey, 24 percent said they knew of instances where therapists abused minor patients. Five percent said they knew of hearsay accounts. Of the fifty-two cases reported, fifty-six percent of the victims were female. Among female victims, the ages ranged from three to seventeen; among male victims the ages ranged from seven to sixteen. Pope went on to say that "studies have shown that an average of one in every 10 male therapists has been involved in at least one incident of intimacy with a patient" (*The Buffalo News,* August 1988, p. A–5).

Why do counselors engage in sexual relations with their clients? What characteristics identify those counselors who are at risk of violating this section of the codes of ethics of their professional organizations? How does it happen?

The following case was described in the *Casebook on Ethical Standards of Psychologists* (1987).

Ms. Y, a former client of Psychologist M, charged him with having engaged in a sexual relationship with her over the course of 18 months, during which period he continued to see her in a client relationship, treating her for depression within the context of marital problems. She accused Psychologist M of seducing her and luring her into an ongoing relationship by waiving fees for treatment and promising to testify for her in child custody hearings. Ms. Y stated that the relationship had been the final blow to her marriage and had cost her custody of her children to her former husband. Furthermore, the relationship had so traumatized her emotionally that she was now again in treatment, attempting to recover.

In response to the Ethics Committee's inquiry, Psychologist M confessed that he was guilty of having a sustained sexual relationship with Ms. Y while she was also his client. However, he claimed that Ms. Y had initiated the sexual contact, and that he had succumbed only after repeated propositions. Within a week of their first sexual encounter he found himself the object of blackmail. Ms. Y threatened him with public exposure, the destruction of his marriage and career, and on one occasion even swore to kill him. Psychologist M begged the Committee to understand that he had lived in constant terror of Ms. Y for a year and a half, continuing their sexual relationship only because the alternative appeared to be the destruction of his life.

After 18 months the guilt and fear proved physically overwhelming and he developed a bleeding ulcer. From his hospital bed he telephoned a prominent local clinician and asked his help. Psychologist M explained that he was now in treatment with Psychologist R, working on countertransference and other issues, and that he had placed his practice under Psychologist R's supervision.

Psychologist M admitted his guilt but begged the Committee members to consider the nightmare he had suffered, the efforts he was making to put his life back together, and the previous 25 years of a spotless career. (APA, 1987, p. 80)

The Ethics Committee found the psychologist guilty of unethical conduct by engaging in sexual intimacies with a client. The Committee was unsympathetic to the psychologist's plea for leniency because of the tragedy that had befallen him. In their words, "this Committee observed that neither the tragic personal consequences of his breach of the ethics code nor the depth of his remorse could absolve him of responsibility for his transgression and for accepting the consequences" (APA, 1987, p. 81). The psychologist was dropped from membership in the American Psychological Association. Unfortunately, this case is not unique.

Butler and Zelen (1977) studied sexual intimacies between therapists and patients of twenty psychiatrists and psychologists who admitted to engaging in sexual contact with their patients. The results of their study indicated that the therapist was usually the aggressor. "In most cases, the therapist, in his leadership role, would bring up the issue of his sexual attraction to the patient. In many cases, the patient responded favorably to these innuendos. Subsequently, there was an acceptance of the mutuality of this attraction and somehow, vaguely, the therapist lost control of the therapeutic hour. The relationship changed from one oriented to therapeutic purposes for the patient alone to one of a more egalitarian relationship where both people were seeking satisfaction in each other. In some situations the therapist's innuendos led to further discussions of the mutual attraction, and then resulted in intercourse. Less productively, other situations occurred in which the therapist's innuendos were almost immediately acted out. In only one instance the patient immediately rejected the proposition and then terminated therapy" (Butler & Zelen, 1977, pp. 141–42).

In a very small number of cases sexual contacts occurred spontaneously. Also, there were a few cases in which sexual relations were prescribed as part of the therapeutic process. Pope and Bouhoutsos (1986) provide what they call ten "varieties" of sexual intimacy between therapist and client. They are: (1) role trading, (2) sex therapy, (3) as if . . . (4) Svengali, (5) drugs, (6) rape, (7) true love, (8) it just got out of hand, (9) time out, and (10) hold me.

Pope and Bouhoutsos (1986) describe *role trading* as follows: "In the same way that in some disturbed family patterns (often involving incest and a similar role in boundary disturbances), the children become 'parents' to their own parents, trying to please and take care of them, some disturbed therapy patterns can involve a reversal of roles. The patient's role is to care for, please, and gratify the wants and needs of the therapist" (p. 6).

The scenario of *sex therapy* involves using sexual intimacy as part of the therapeutic process. Sexual contact with patients is advocated as a controversial form of therapeutic modality. Herman et al. in 1978 surveyed 5,574 randomly selected psychiatrists with a thirty-four-item questionnaire about sexual contact between patient and therapist. They found that less than 2 percent of the respondents believed "that such (sexual) contact could be appropriate for enhancement of the patient's self-esteem, as a corrective emotional experience for the patient, to shorten a grief reaction, or to convert a patient from one sexual orientation to another" (p. 165).

The *as if* . . . scenario of sexual relations between a counselor and a client occurs when the client finds the counselor sexually attractive. The scenario that develops is just "as if . . ." the patient were falling in love with the counselor outside the therapeutic relationship. Again Pope and Bouhoutsos (1986) comment that "patients frequently believe that they have fallen in love with their therapists. It is frequently a normal part of therapy. But therapists are supposed to be trained to resist, no matter how seductive the patient becomes" (p. 4).

In the scenario of *Svengali,* counselors become powerful charismatic figures to the clients. Almost in a cult-like fashion, clients come to worship their counselors with a bond so strong that the clients act in a manner totally out of character with their normal behavior. "The sexual intimacies between therapist and patient may take on the trappings of a religious ritual, and may eventually involve three or more people" (Pope & Bouhoutsos, 1986, p. 12).

The scenarios of *drugs* and *rape* represent examples of counselors who use drugs to make their clients vulnerable to sexual exploitation. Rape, as used by Pope and Bouhoutsos, refers to the criminal act of forcing someone to engage involuntarily in sexual relations. Some writers suggest that any time a counselor engages in sexual intercourse with a client it should be deemed rape, because of the vulnerability of the client, even if the client has given consent.

Another scenario suggested by Pope and Bouhoutsos (1986) is called *true love.* In this scenario, counselors believe that they have fallen in love with their clients; they neither believe that they are sexually exploiting the clients nor that they are doing anything unethical. Quite the contrary, a deep personal love is thought to exist. The counseling relationship may even end while the counselors continue the romantic relationship with their clients.

Falling in love is the most common explanation given by counselors to explain sexual relations with their clients. Butler and Zelen (1977) reported that of the twenty therapists they surveyed who had engaged in sexual intimacies with their clients, 55 percent said that relations resulted from their "total attraction to their patients." They quote one therapist as saying, "I would have liked her just as much if I had met her anywhere else" (p. 142). Unfortunately, he did not meet her anywhere else. He met her during a therapy session.

Pope and Bouhoutsos (1986) use strong words in commenting on the ethics of a counselor who justifies having sexual relations with his client by arguing that he had just "fallen in love." "The inventive mind of the therapist never need run short of rationalization for engaging in unprincipled behavior. 'True love' is among the most powerful, seductive, and chronic of these justifications. Once a therapist believes 'true love' exists, all possible objections fall helpless before its awesome and mysterious sway. 'True love' is its own justification and a seeming justification for all things. It makes 'all fair'. Like the Lorelei, 'true love' lures the therapy off course toward untold destruction. It is only later, when the spell fades, that the true horrors of the consequences begin to make themselves known" (p. 16).

How is it that persons so highly trained in interpersonal skills should be vulnerable to "falling in love" with their clients? Counselors do not deliberately set out to violate the ethical principles of their profession. They find that suddenly during the course of the counseling session something special emerges. As Pope and Bouhoutsos (1986) indicate in their scenario, as clients begin to reveal things about themselves, counselors may become infatuated or in awe of their clients' inner strength of character. The relationship suddenly shifts in the mind of the counselor to one of a nonprofessional nature between two peers, where each is spoken of in a special way. Counselors so affected begin to share their own innermost thoughts and fears with clients. Soon the relationship is taken outside the office.

As mentioned earlier, many counselors do recognize their ethical responsibility and terminate the counseling relationship. However, they continue the social relationship which ultimately leads to sexual intimacies with the client. Perr (1975) and Marnor (1972), reported in Herman et al. (1987), argue that "falling in love" should be an exception to the prohibition against sexual relations with clients. Yet, Marnor agrees that there are several reasons to ban sexual relations with clients. He writes, "I must still affirm my clinical conviction that the therapist to whom this happens has failed in his primary responsibility to the woman who came to him as a patient. I make this statement in full knowledge of the fact that a number of prominent psychiatrists and psychoanalysts have married former patients. How many others, who did not reach this honorable endpoint, have nevertheless rationalized their loss of self-control on the basis of 'falling in love' with their patients I do not know. My point, however, is that such a rationalization should not obscure the fact that whenever this happens, the psychotherapist has not been able to master his countertransference feelings" (Herman et al., 1987, p. 168).

All sexual relations with a client are unethical. Professional codes of conduct make no provision for a counselor falling in love with his client.

Numerous authors have argued that the prohibition against sexual intimacies with former clients should be just as strong as the prohibition against sexual relations with current clients (Anderson cited in Herman et al., 1987; Brodsky, cited in Herman et al., 1987; Sell, Gottlieb & Schoen-feld, 1986; ECAPA. 1988; Pope & Bouhoutsos, 1986).

☞ In the scenario *It just got out of hand,* the client seduces the therapist. There is no question who is culpable. While recognizing that patients frequently believe that they have fallen in love with their therapist, Pope comments, "It is very frequently a normal part of therapy, but therapists are supposed to be trained to resist no matter how seductive a patient becomes" (*The Buffalo News,* August 1988, p. A-5).

⤳ In the scenario of *time out* Pope and Bouhoutsos (1986) posit the situation in which the psychologist separates what happens "on the job" from what happens "off the job." For example, a casual lunch with a client leads to a sexual involvement. The therapist rationalizes the act because the sexual intimacy occurred outside of the therapy sessions. Pope and Bouhoutsos's (1986) description of the reaction of the hypothetical client is particularly informative. They write: "After three months of sexual in-volvement, Reve abruptly drops out of the therapy group and discontinues all involvement with her therapist. She moves to another city and manages to hold herself together for two years, virtually wiping out all active memory of her intimacy with Dr. Quincy. Over the course of the next year, she gradually begins to decompensate and loses her job. She is hospitalized after a psychotic break. Discharged from the hospital, she begins a long course of therapy and after three years of work, becomes able to acknowl-edge the devastating impact her sexual involvement with her therapist had caused" (p. 19).

The ethical prohibition against sexual relations with clients is analogous to that of the incest taboo. In exploring this analogy, Brodsky comments, "Father-daughter incest does not become acceptable one year after the daughter has left home. No matter how the therapy contact ends, the imbalance of power of the initial interactions can never be erased" (Herman et al., 1987, p. 168). Thus, therapist/client sexual intimacy does not become acceptable once the professional relationship ends. Sell et al. (1986) reflect the broadly held opinion about sexual relations with former clients: "We contend that sexual relations with former clients are exploitive and unethical if they follow any therapeutic relationship, regardless of the lapsed time period. . . . We believe that the only way to address the problem of psychiatrists who are sexually involved with former clients is to prohibit post-treatment sexual relations altogether" (p. 507). They go on to recom-mend that Ethical Principle 6.a. of the APA Standards be amended to prohibit sexual intimacies both with clients and former clients.

Some state legislatures already provide leadership in this area. For example, the State of Florida prohibits sexual relations between a psychiatrist and a client in perpetuity (Florida Chapter 21U-15.004). In California, damages for sexual relations with a client are recoverable against the therapist for a period of two years following termination of psychotherapy (California Civil Code, Section 43.93). Sell, Schoenfeld, and Gottlieb (1986) surveyed "the chairpersons of state and provincial ethics committees and executive directors of licensing boards" to determine "the frequency of complaints of sexual impropriety filed against psychologists during 1982 and 1983." They found that "psychologists asserting that a sexual relationship had occurred only after the termination of a therapeutic relationship were more likely to be found in violation than those not making the claim" (p. 504).

The final scenario is termed *hold me*. In this example, the therapist "exploits the patient's deep and overwhelming desire to be held and comforted" (Pope & Bouhoutsos, 1986, p. 21).

Why do counselors engage in sexual relations with their clients? Chesler (1972) interviewed two therapists who had repeatedly engaged in sexual relations with their clients. These professionals described their wives as "crazy," "hopeless," "dependent," and "too old" (p. 150). The therapists' own personal needs and motivations overwhelmingly contributed to the sexual contact in that the therapists acknowledged their needs as a factor in this sexual behavior" (Butler & Zelen, 1987, p. 142). Butler and Zelen found that of the twenty participants who acknowledged sexual relationships, 90 percent reported to have been "vulnerable, needy, and/or lonely." These researchers (1987) postulate that one might "assume the therapists shifted their sources of gratification to their patients during vulnerable or needy periods of time. Therapists who had more than one experience initiated the sexual contacts during their needy times." Butler and Zelen went on to remark that "it is possible to construe the same theory of neurotic behavior for these therapists that they may have done for so many of their patients, that their own neurotic maelstroms led to non-therapeutic behavior. These results . . . further validate the assumption that these clinicians did not act as therapists. Rather they were engaged in self-serving, need-fulfilling behavior which had high reinforcement value" (1987, p. 142).

Holroyd, Haransky, and Brodsky (1977) conducted a nation-wide survey of psychologists' attitudes and practices regarding erotic and non-erotic contact with patients, the conclusions of which support the findings of Butler and Zelen. Some of the written comments they received are revealing. "I feel without qualification that erotic patient-therapist contact is unethical at best and devastating at worst:—it reflects pathological needs on the part of the therapist"; and "literal mindedness and a paucity of imagination on the part of the therapist (or a badly functioning personal life) would explain but not ever justify sexual or quasi-erotic contact with patients"; and "when is the wedding between psychology and prostitution going to take place?" (p. 848).

Most authors conclude that sexual relations with clients reflect the antithesis of everything that helping professions stand for. "It undermines the integrity of the profession" (Pope, *The Buffalo News* [August 1988], p. A-5). For counselors, this activity may result in arrest for rape or child abuse, disruption of career, major awards of damages for malpractice (including one of more than $2 million), revocation of license, the end of a marriage, deepseated feelings of guilt and conflict, and possibly even suicide, could also result. "For the patient the negative effects were excessive conflict, destructive experience, and psychological pain" (Holroyd & Brodsky, 1977, p. 848). Among the negative effects identified by the Butler and Zelen (1977) survey were "the inequality between the participants, particularly in relation to the powerful role of the therapist, the tremendous conflicts experienced by both, and especially the eventual feelings of anger, hurt and damage to the patient after the relationship had resolved" (p. 144).

Of the eleven women who had sexual relations with their therapists, Chesler (1972) discovered during his interviews that "one woman tried to kill herself; two others lapsed into a severe depression; a fourth woman's husband, who was also in treatment with the same therapist, killed himself shortly after finding out about the affair" (p. 147). Chesler also reports that the "therapist's rather sadistic and grandiose attempt to cure this woman's (the man's wife) 'frigidity' one night resulted in her developing a 'headache' that wouldn't subside for a year" (p. 147).

The consequences for the client can be deep, devastating, and long-lasting. "A final argument against sexual involvement with clients is that they often feel taken advantage of and may discount the value of any part of their therapy. They may become embittered and angry, and they may terminate therapy with psychological scars. The problem is compounded if they are deterred from initiating therapy with anyone else because of the traumatic experience and thus feel stuck with their unresolved feelings" (Corey, Corey & Callanan, 1984, p. 215).

What should a counselor do who experiences a desire to become sexually involved with a client? First, discuss the situation with a colleague. Butler and Zelen (1977) found that while 90 percent of the twenty psychotherapists they interviewed reported a conflict, fearing guilt about having sexual relations with their patients, less than 40 percent sought consultation. Second, terminate the counseling relationship. Butler and Zelen (1977) found that less than half the therapists who found themselves in potentially compromising situations chose to end the counseling relationship.

The counseling professions can take a number of steps to deal with this problem, steps which include publishing sanctions brought by professional societies against individuals who engage in sexual relations with their clients. Mandating curriculum reform in college programs to require a course in ethics would reinforce the concern for professional propriety. Modifying course content to specifically address sexual relations with clients might prove beneficial. Moreover, the counseling professions should make a stronger statement in their codes of ethics prohibiting, under any circumstances, sexual intimacies with both current clients *and* former clients.

REFERENCES

American Psychological Association. 1981. "Ethical Principles of Psychologists," *American Psychologist* **36,** 633–38.

American Psychological Association. 1987. *Casebook on Ethical Standards of Psychologists,* Washington, D.C.: American Psychological Association, Inc.

The Buffalo News. 1988. (August), p. A–5.

Butler, S., and Zelen, S. L. 1977. "Sexual Intimacies Between Therapists and Patients," *Psychotherapy Theory Research and Practice,* **14** (2), 139.

California Civil Code. 1989. Section 43.93 (West Supp.).

Chesler, P. 1972. *Women and Madness,* New York: Doubleday and Company.

Corey, G.; Corey, M. S.; and Callanan P. 1984. *Issues and Ethics in the Helping Professions,* Monterey, Calif.: Brooks Cole Publishing Company.

Ethics Committee, American Psychological Association (ECAPA). 1988. "Trends in Ethics Cases, Common Pitfalls in Published Resources," *American Psychologist* **7,** 567.

Etziony, M. D. 1973. *The Physician's Creed,* Springfield, Mass.: Charles Thomas.

Florida Administrative Code 21U-15.004 (1988).

Herman, J. L.; Jartrell, N.; Olarte, S.; Feldstein, M.; and Localio, R. February 1987. "Psychiatrist-Patient Sexual Conduct: Results of a

National Survey, 2: Psychiatrists' Attitudes," *American Journal of Psychiatry* **114** (2), 164.

Holroyd, J. C., and Brodsky, A. M. 1977. "Psychologists' Attitudes and Practices Regarding Erotic and Neurotic Physical Contact with Patients," *American Psychologist* **32,** 843.

Pope, K. S., and Bouhoutsos J. C. 1986. *Sexual Intimacy Between Therapist and Patients,* New York: Praeger Publishers.

Sell, J. M.; Gottlieb, M. C.; and Schoenfeld, L. 1986. "Ethical Considerations of Social/Romantic Relations with Present and Former Clients," *Professional Psychology Research and Practice* **17** (6), 504.

9

Working with Women

A very successful female executive arrives for a job interview, and is met by an all-male panel, one of whose members asks, "You have a reputation for being assertive. How do you explain it?" The clear implication of this question is that (*a*) assertiveness in a woman is bad; (*b*) because assertiveness in a woman is bad, it needs to be justified; and (*c*) the woman has probably advanced as far as she has *because* of this negative personality trait.

The following examples are used by women executives to illustrate society's double standard when describing successful male and female executives. A male executive is viewed as dynamic, fair, good in details, has the courage of his convictions, and is human; a female executive with these same traits is described as aggressive, inflexible, picky, stubborn, and emotional. These statements are used to demonstrate that the same personality traits considered as attributes in males are renamed and considered as liabilities in females.

While most professionals would deplore sexual stereotyping in general, many fail to recognize that they are guilty of unethical behavior by practicing sex-role stereotyping as counselors.

Do counselors sex-role stereotype their clients, and, if so, what can be done to change this behavior? Broverman et al. (1970) undertook break-through research on sex bias and sex-role stereotyping by counselors. This often-cited study (see also Broverman et al., 1972) found that what was considered to be healthy behavior in males was viewed by mental health workers to be pathological behavior in women. The research also found that "behavior attributes which are regarded as healthy for an adult, sex unspecified, and thus presumably viewed from an ideal, absolute standpoint, will more often be considered by clinicians as more healthy or appropriate for men than for women" (Broverman et al., 1970, p. 1).

Broverman et al. (1970) developed a questionnaire of bi-polar items that describe particular behavior traits or characteristics, some of which could be characterized as typically masculine and the others typically feminine. Then 79 male and female clinical psychologists, psychiatrists, and social workers were asked to verify those characteristics most typical of "a mature, healthy, socially adjusted, competent adult male" (17 men and 10 women), those typical of a "mature, healthy, socially competent adult female" (14 men and 12 women), and, finally, those of a "healthy, mature, socially competent adult person" of unspecified sex (15 men and 11 women). The researchers found that there was general agreement on the characteristics of a healthy male, healthy female, and healthy adult of unspecified sex. Furthermore, they found that these characteristics were different for men and women, and that these "differences parallel the sex-role stereotypes prevalent in our society" (Broverman et al., 1970, p. 5). Broverman et al. concluded that a dangerous double standard existed: traits that clinicians would normally ascribe to healthy adults were those they would only ascribe to males, while a different set of traits, those perceived to be less healthy or even unhealthy, were ascribed to females. "For instance, among these items, clinicians are more likely to suggest that healthy women differ from healthy men by being more submissive, less independent, less adventurous, more easily influenced, less aggressive, less competitive, more excitable in minor crises, having their feelings more easily hurt, being more emotional, more conceited about their appearance, less objective, and disliking math and science. This constellation seems a most unusual way of describing any mature, healthy individual" (Broverman et al., 1970, pp. 4–5).

Broverman postulated that the most likely cause of the apparent double standard rises from the clinician's notion of how women have adjusted to their environment and the social roles they play in our society. "An adjustment notion of health, plus the existence of differential norms of male and female behavior in our society, automatically leads to a double standard of health. Thus, for a women to be healthy, from an adjustment viewpoint, she must adjust to and accept the behavioral norms of her sex, even though these behaviors are generally less socially desirable and considered to be less healthy for the generalized, competent, mature adult" (Broverman et al., 1970, p. 6).

Recent studies have continued to confirm the findings of Broverman's (1970) original study. For example, Page (1987) found that "this recent evidence . . . does, however, affirm once more the essential validity of the original Broverman et al. study. Social and clinical judgments do appear to be affected, not only by the seriousness of the unacceptable behavior, but also by the degree of congruity with prevailing gender role stereotypes. The trend for this to apply more strongly to male nonconformity appears also to support the claims of Broverman et al. that females tend to be seen as 'by nature' less than mentally healthy and as persons in whom maladjustment is considered intrinsic and thus less problematic or important" (pp. 57–58).

Sex-role stereotyping affects counselors' judgments about the mental health of clients, their practice of counseling, and their ethical conduct as counselors. In chapter 2 justice was set forth as one of the principles underlying the ethical practices of counselors. Justice in its broader sense means fairness. In the classical Aristotelian sense, justice meant treating equals equally and unequals unequally; however, we are only justified in treating people unequally if the nature of the inequality is relevant to the issue in our case (Edwards, 1967). It would appear, therefore, that no compelling reason exists to justify treating females differently than males in psychotherapy, career counseling, and most (if not all) other aspects of counseling. The just practice of counselors is reinforced not only in law, but in the statement of ethics and professional standards of the professional organizations: "Members perform in a fashion that is not discriminatory on the basis of race, sex, national origin, affectional/sexual preference, handicap, age, or creed, and they work actively to modify discriminatory practices when encountered" (Callis et al., 1982, p. 166).

Unfortunately, there is good evidence to conclude that sex-role stereotyping continues to be a problem for the counseling profession. In a review of sexist/practices in the helping professions, Nickerson (1979) found that, unlike their male counterparts, females fail to receive the same quality of service from members of the mental health professions. "Contemporary therapists and counselors, for the most part, fare no better, as abundant evidence of sexism has been documented in studies indicating differential diagnosis, expectations, and treatment of the sexes by present-day breathing and practicing helpers" (p. 5).

Vocational and guidance counselors continue to be surprised and uneasy when a female client expresses an interest in pursuing a nontraditional occupation field. Vocational choices such as fireman, policeman, or welder continue to be looked upon with skepticism and even disfavor and disdain by counselors. Guidance counselors continue to caution women about pursuing careers in fields that require sophisticated mathematical skills. Consequently, only 4.4 percent of the Ph.D. degrees awarded in engineering in 1987 went to females. The numbers are even smaller for computer science. The problem is similar for other counseling fields.

Sexual stereotyping in counseling has other ethical consequences for counseling behavior. It forces and reinforces women into "traditional" social roles and, as we have already seen, into unhealthy patterns of behavior (Hutt, 1979). It reinforces unhealthy feelings when women choose non-traditional roles and behave in nontraditional patterns. Sex-role bias may cause counselors to "misidentify or erroneously regard as psychiatric disturbance subject to intervention by psychotherapy or clinical treatment" women's problems in living, which in reality may be a result of socio-economic, ethical, or legal conditions (Hare-Muslin, 1983, p. 593). At the same time, because of the double standard of mental health, counselors may fail to identify and treat appropriate problems that are peculiar to women. "Women have been too long neglected or relegated to a second-class delivery of less-than-second-class mental health services" (Nickerson, 1979, p. 5).

What can counselors do to change sex-role bias when working with female clients? A significant first step would be to increase the number of women who choose the profession of counseling. While women make up the majority of clients seen by counselors, almost all the counseling professions are male dominated. This becomes even more true at the management levels. One reason there are not more women entering the counseling professions is that, traditionally, marriage serves as a disincentive for these professions, as it does for most professional fields. "Married female psychologists increase their workload by about two full work days a week as a result of marriage, while male psychologists reduce their workload by about three days per week when they marry" (Williams et al., 1980, p. 100).

Second, counselors can use their special positions in society to change the sex-role stereotypes cited by Broverman et al. (1970): "Clinicians undoubtedly exert an influence on social standards and attitudes beyond that of other groups. This influence arises not only from their effect on many individuals through conventional clinical functioning, but also out of their role as 'expert,' which leads to consultation to government, private agencies of all kinds, as well as guidance to the general public" (pp. 6–7).

Counselors must become better aware of their own values and assumptions toward women and understand how these values and assumptions can bias and restrict their ability to deliver quality care to their female clients. Counselors who work with women need to understand the unique biological, psychological, and social issues involved in counseling women. "Women report more worries and say more often than do men that they have felt that they were going to have a nervous breakdown. Women say more frequently that bad things happen to them more often and feel overwhelmed by bad events that happen. They experience more feelings of inadequacy as parents, report slightly more psychological anxiety, and endorse slightly lower self-evaluations and personal efficacy statements than do men" (Russo, 1985, p. 5).

The education of counselors includes not only an obligation to understand the real differences between men and women, but to ferret out and destroy the artificial and contrived ones. Graduate programs for counselors need to be modified to offer adequate and full discussion of the ethical standards for nonsexist practice. Students need to understand that sex bias is antithetical to the fundamental principles of counseling, viz., to do good and to prevent harm. Counselors have an affirmative obligation to weed out the underlying causes of sex biases within their ranks and to develop new practices that promote the health of their female clients. In the words of Hare-Muslin (1983), "As women's half-known lives become better known, the old myths, traditional expectations, inadequate and inappropriate treatment, and conformity to sex-role stereotypes will no longer be accepted as the basis for the psychotherapy of women" (Hare-Muslin, p. 599).

REFERENCES

Broverman, D.; Broverman, I.; Clarkson, F.; Rosencrantz, P.; and Vogel, S. 1970. "Sex Role Stereotypes and Clinical Judgments of Mental Health," *Journal of Counseling and Clinical Psychology* **24**, 1-7.

Broverman, D.; Broverman, I.; Clarkson, F.; Rosencrantz, P.; and Vogel, S. 1972. "Sexual Stereotypes: A Current Appraisal," *Journal of Social Issues,* **28**, 59.

Callis, R.; Pope, S. K.; and Depauw, M. E. 1982. *Ethical Standards Casebook,* Falls Church, Va.: American Personnel and Guidance Journal.

Edwards, P. 1967. *The Encyclopedia of Philosophy,* New York: Macmillan.

Hare-Muslin, R. T. 1983. "An Appraisal of the Relationship Between Women and Psychotherapy," *American Psychologist* **38** (5), 593.

Hutt, R. L. 1979. "Review and Preview of Attitudes and Values of Counselors of Women," *Counseling Psychologist* **8** (1), 18.

Nickerson, E. T. 1979. "How Helpful are the Helpers? A Selected Review of Sexist Helping Practices," *Counseling Psychologist* **8** (1), 85.

Page, S. 1987. "On Gender Roles and Perception of Maladjustment," *Canadian Psychology* **28** (1), 53.

Russo, N. F. (ed.). 1985. *A Women's Mental Health Agenda,* Washington, D.C.: American Psychological Association.

Williams, T. M.; Zorbrock, M. L.; and Harrison, L. F. 1980. "Some Factors Affecting Women's Participation in Psychology in Canada," *Canadian Psychology* **21**, 97.

10

Lying and Deception

One of the most fundamental ethical principles of an effective counselor-client relationship is veracity; the relationship builds upon an ethical bond of honesty, integrity, candor, and truthfulness. As a general rule, the relationship is seriously undermined when either of the parties engages in deception or lying.

Bok (1978) defines a lie as "any intentionally deceptive message which is stated" (p. 13). A lie may be either spoken or written. Regardless of the form it takes, there must be a clear intent by the author to deceive the person receiving the information. This form of lying is termed a "lie of commission" because an affirmative act has been committed. I will argue that there is another form of lying called the "lie of omission." This lie occurs when the counselor deliberately allows another person to believe that information is true when in fact the counselor knows it to be false. Intentionally allowing a client to believe something that the counselor knows to be false, and not bringing this fact to the client's attention, is as much a deliberate act of deception as a lie of commission.

Deception is a much broader category because it involves both intentionally deceptive statements and deceptive acts. Synonyms for deception include double-dealing, trickery, subterfuge, and fraud.

Why do people lie and practice deception? The most common reason given is that those who lie are really performing an act of kindness. Consider the following case: You are a seventeen-year veteran counselor in an agency that serves infants and children who suffer from severe multiple physical handicaps. Two months ago the Smedleys registered their nine-month-old son, Bobby, on the advice and recommendation of a pediatrician. Bobby is the Smedleys' only child. You have had numerous occasions during the past two months to observe Bobby as well as discuss his case on a regular basis with his physical therapist and the agency's consulting pediatrician. All who have observed Bobby conclude that not only is he severely physically handicapped but severely mentally retarded as well.

One day the Smedleys come to you and, during casual conversation, they remark that "it is tough to have a handicapped child." They have struggled at great length with the problem, not only between themselves but also with members of their family. The Smedleys have finally come to accept the fact that Bobby is severely physically handicapped. But the one thing they know they could never accept, and "thank God, will never have to accept," is the fact that he would be mentally retarded. They then turn to you in a questioning fashion and say, "Thank God, isn't it wonderful that he is not also mentally retarded."

How do you respond? You appear to have two options. First, confirm the parents' statement that, "yes, it is wonderful that he is not mentally retarded," or second, you could, with great skill, say to them that "we need to talk about this because, based upon our observations and our experience, your son appears to be mentally retarded, though it is too early to tell the extent of it."

You decide to lie to the Smedleys because you think it would be an act of kindness and, in your opinion, in the best interests of your clients. You reached this conclusion for the followings reasons: There is probably very little that the Smedleys can do to change the reality that their son is mentally retarded; therefore, living a little longer with this myth would not do any harm and certainly would not affect the development of the child. In fact, it may be good for the Smedleys to have a little longer to adjust to the situation that their baby is not normal and to have an opportunity to develop additional support systems to deal with this fact as well as to address the grief of the family members, which many times develops in situations such as this.

Also, perhaps it is not your job to tell them. Certainly, as the child gets older, it should become more obvious to the parents that their child is mentally retarded and, therefore, the best approach is for them to discover this for themselves. So, with a little luck, you should probably be able to dodge the problem altogether.

It might be argued that this case is similar to the act of kindness that causes one not to tell a dying patient that she is dying. Using similar reasoning, a counselor might decide not to tell a patient she is dying because it would not change the circumstances of her death. Also, it might be in the patient's best interest to let her enjoy her remaining time without being needlessly confused or caused unnecessary pain and suffering (Bok, 1978).

Letters of recommendation written on behalf of students and employees by counselors are often cited as another act of lying out of kindness (Bok, 1978). The reasoning runs something like the following: In this day and age there are only two types of recommendations—good recommendations and great recommendations. Since the system has become so inflated, the counselor feels obligated to compensate by supplying the client with an exaggerated recommendation. The counselor reasons that the lie is justified because he is only acting on the best interests of the student by "leveling the playing field."

Another explanation offered for why people lie is that it prevents harm. The best example of this is lying to an enemy in war. In this instance, the lie is justified because it saves lives and saves the country from some evil, in this case the enemy. For the counselor, there may be an occasion to lie to save a life. For example, a crisis intervention counselor or hotline operator may stretch the bounds of truth when a person calls and threatens suicide. The caller says he will carry out the act unless the counselor gets hold of the individual's parent. The counselor may deceive the caller into believing that the parent is being summoned while stealing precious moments necessary for the police to respond.

Another, less magnanimous reason for lying is to achieve personal gain. The counselor may exaggerate his credentials in a brochure soliciting clients for his consulting business. It is important to note that many times what is represented as a lie for the public good is, in reality, a lie for private gain. In the words of Bok (1978), "We cannot take for granted either the altruism or the good judgment of those who lie to us, no matter how much they intend to benefit us. We have learned that much deceit for private gain masquerades as being in the public interest" (p. 169).

Finally, fear is often given as a justification for lying. For example, a person may lie because he is afraid of what other people may think of him if he told the truth. This explanation is often used to justify exaggerations. Lies are often perpetrated out of fear; the consequences of telling the truth may be too great. We may lie to escape punishment for doing something wrong, or we may lie to escape involvement in an awkward or unpleasant situation.

Some counselors claim that it is not wrong to lie because they possess a certain professional license that frees them from ordinary moral constraints when they are in the service of clients. In essence, it is all right to lie if it improves the counseling relationship. In the words of a colleague who wished to remain anonymous, "Other professionals regard fabricated disclosures as merely a synthesis of life experiences tailored to a particular situation and, therefore, not deception but a method of enhancing communication in the counseling relationship."

One interesting point about lying and deception is that when the counselor chooses to lie rather than tell the truth, he feels morally obligated to defend his action to himself and/or to others. While the truth needs no defense (Bok, 1978), a lie always needs to be defended as just, right, or proper by providing adequate reasons. The reasons counselors offer for choosing to lie or use deception rather than telling the truth are many and varied. First, since it is the job of the counselor to help the client, the counselor may decide to lie because the falsehood is in the best interest of the client. This is a "means/ends" argument, where the lie (the means) becomes justified by the result (the end) it creates. For example, a counselor might argue that he was justified in lying to a client if to do so helped the client deal with a problem or was in keeping with the counselor's higher obligation to protect the client's rights; for example, in protecting the client's right to confidentiality. Certainly we can think of cases where such justification is valid, such as in instances where a lie saves a life.

However, all too often this justification is used in cases where it is not clear that the end would not have resulted without the lie, or where the lie actually created more harm than good. Nonetheless, this justification is the most common rationale offered by counselors when confronted with having lied.

Other justifications offered in defense of lying include the argument that the agency or individual would not understand the information or would misuse it if provided; therefore, the counselor is justified in lying or withholding information. A parallel argument offered by counselors is that clients or parents really cannot handle the truth; therefore, the counselor is acting in their best interest (albeit paternalistically) by feeding them information that the counselor believes they can handle, i.e., a lie. Sometimes telling the truth is dismissed by the counselor on the grounds that it really will not do any good; therefore, it does not really matter. Conversely, counselors may justify lying because it does not cause harm. As Bok (1978) points out, it is naive and foolish to believe that lying does not cause harm.

Sometimes a justification for lying is offered on the grounds that the counselor has been forced into the situation. In this instance, we might hear such statements as, "Sure, I lied. What do you expect from me? I didn't want to get involved in the first place." Or, "Sure, I lied, but only because you made me do something that wasn't in my job description." In this justification, the counselor shifts the blame or guilt to the supervisor or colleague since, the counselor argues, it is permissible to lie when one has been mistreated or has had one's rights violated—i.e., as a result of coercion.

Finally, a justification may be offered in the form of using a lie to educate the victim or to get revenge: "It's all right to lie to a liar because he's only getting what he deserves."

The counselor may in fact lie or deceive on behalf of the client. These acts of deception usually take the form of letters of recommendation, reports to other agencies, parents, or reports to students. A counselor may also lie to or deceive his supervisor or employer regarding absenteeism, lack of productivity, or personal problems that affect job performance. Supervisors may lie to or deceive counselors when doing evaluations and in telling the counselor why the supervisor is upset.

THE HARM IN LYING AND DECEPTION

As we have seen, one of the justifications given by a person who lies or deceives is that the lie or deception has not caused any harm. Bok (1978) has identified a number of harms that result from lies and deceit. A lie hurts the liar by reducing the confidence of clients and peers. The counselor who lies fears getting caught. This fear produces vulnerability and could even lead to treachery or blackmail. Lies hurt, then, because they isolate the liar. A lie biases the counselor's judgment by making it appear as though lying is a viable option for extricating oneself from a tight spot. Eventually, greater risks are taken on the naïve assumption that one more lie will remove the danger.

Perhaps the most insidious effect of lying is the freedom it robs from the person on whom the lie is perpetrated. The liar's victims are unable to make choices for themselves according to the most accurate information available. They are unable to act as they would have wanted to act had they known the truth (Bok, 1978). In fact, the lie may cause a client to choose some detrimental course of action, which most probably would not have been chosen had the truth been known (Steininger et al., 1984).

Besides reducing one's range of choices, lying is coercive. It takes power away from the victim and gives it to the liar. Lying enables the perpetrator to manipulate the behavior of his victim. This is an excellent example of the old adage "Knowledge is power."

Finally, lying can undermine and destroy the counseling relationship and ultimately undermine the credibility of the profession of counseling in the public's eye.

It is not my intention to suggest that there are no circumstances in which it would be appropriate for the counselor to lie. Such a statement would be naïve and foolish. In fact, Bok (1978) offers a test to determine the circumstances in which it would be appropriate to lie rather than tell the truth.

When considering deception, counselors should ask themselves two questions: (1) Could a truthful alternative to lying be chosen? If so, then counselors should choose to tell the truth rather than lie. Engaging in a lie should be done only as a last resort (Bok, 1978). (2) What moral arguments can be made for and against the choice to lie in the specific situation? Counselors need to consider carefully the justifications put forth in defense of lying. They should ask themselves several important questions: Are these justifications adequate? Are they defensible? Do the arguments in favor of the lie clearly and convincingly outweigh those against the lie?

Finally, the decision to lie should only be made after applying Bok's "Test of Publicity," which requires that counselors ask what the public's reaction would be if society knew that counselors had chosen to lie over telling the truth, given the specific circumstances of some case. In a sense, Bok has suggested a reasonable-man standard to guide counselors in assessing the appropriateness of choosing to lie over telling the truth. If the public would accept and understand the choice to lie rather than tell the truth, then the counselor's decision to lie would be justified. "We must share the perspective of those affected by our choices, and ask how we would react if the lies we are contemplating were told to us. We must, then, adopt the perspective not only of liars but of those lied to; and not only of particular persons but of all those affected by lies—the collective perspective of reasonable persons seen as potentially deceived. We must formulate the excuses and the moral arguments used to defend the lies and ask how they would stand up under the public scrutiny of these reasonable persons" (Bok, 1978, p. 93).

REFERENCES

Bok, S. 1978. *Lying: Moral Choice in Public and Private Life,* New York: Pantheon Books.

Steininger M.; Newell, J. D.; and Garcia, L. T. 1984, *Ethical Issues in Psychology,* Homewood, Ill.: Dorsey Press.

11

Paternalism

Sometimes counselors find themselves in the unique role of acting on their clients' behalf. In other words, counselors may be called upon or feel compelled to act paternalistically when a client is unable to give informed consent, as in the case of children or the developmentally disabled. They may feel a responsibility to protect clients from harm or to prevent clients from harming others.

Gert and Culver (1975) insist on a rigorous definition of paternalism. They argue that the following necessary conditions must be present if a counselor's actions are to be properly termed paternalistic: (1) the counselor believes that his action will benefit his client; (2) the counselor does not have the client's permission to act on his behalf; (3) the client has chosen a course of action that he believes is best; (4) the counselor's action violates the client's rights; and (5) the counselor's action is justified by the good it creates for the client.

I find Gert and Culver's definition a bit too restrictive; I would allow that a counselor is acting paternalistically even if he has his client's permission. In such an instance the counselor will act for the client when the client cannot act for himself.

Casting counselors in a paternalistic role raises certain ethical problems, including bringing into conflict the counselor's obligation to promote client autonomy and the concomitant obligation to act beneficently toward the client. The following case is illustrative:

> Carlos was a 13-year-old Hispanic boy brought in to treatment by his mother because he was in danger of being expelled from school and had become virtually uncontrollable at home. He lived with his mother and two-year-old sister in a small apartment. He was hostile and evasive in the initial session which was also attended by his mother. She was explicit about the fact that she wanted the therapist to talk to Carlos and "straighten him out." In particular, with Carlos out of the room, she confided to the therapist that she had had enough of the boy and wanted the therapist to persuade him to go to live with his father. She reported that Carlos was completely against the idea, but felt she could no longer handle the strain and felt it was in his best interest. She asked the therapist to persuade the boy. (Powell, 1984, p. 63)

The first ethical question that arises is: Does the counselor have the right to act paternalistically toward his client? The counseling profession's code of ethics recognizes certain classes of clients who are not in a position to act on their own behalf. The *Ethical Principles of Psychologists,* Principle 5.d., states: "When working with minors or other persons who are unable to give voluntary, informed consent, psychologists take special care to protect these persons' best interest" (APA, 1981, p. 636).

While professional associations clearly recognize that under certain circumstances it is appropriate and necessary for counselors to act paternalistically toward clients, how do counselors determine what those circumstances are? Counselors who find themselves in potential paternalistic situations should ask two questions: (1) Is the request in the best interest of my client? and (2) What is the potential harm that might occur if the client were free to make an independent decision?

The first question arises from the counselor's ethical obligation to act only in ways that benefit the client. As mentioned earlier by Kitchener (1984), counselors have a duty to act in ways that promote the client's good. Paternalism, on its face, would appear to be a malevolent act because it denies to clients the right to control their own lives or some significant portion thereof. In order for counselors to demonstrate that they are acting beneficently, they would need to assert that without the contemplated intervention essential harm would come to the client because he is not competent to make an informed choice. Therefore, in answering the above two questions, if counselors conclude that the potential for harm exceeds the potential for good, they would be justified in imposing their will on the client.

How does a counselor justify acting paternalistically? Gert and Culver (1975) suggest application of the following test. Can it be claimed that any rational person would agree that the counselor acted properly and, furthermore, that the counselor could publicly state that any one of his peers, if confronted with the same situation, would act the same? I recommend that in addition to applying this test, counselors should also ask themselves the following questions: (1) Could the client have acted independently to further his own interest? (2) If the client could have been free to act and could have made a rational choice, would that choice have been the one made by the counselor? (3) From the client's perspective, did the counselor's act result in more good than harm?

Powell (1984) concluded that "ethical considerations appear to bind the psychologist to say no to the mother's request in this particular case. The psychologist would appear to be serving the best interests of everyone and acting most ethically by offering the mother the possibility of working the issue through with Carlos. He or she would also need to make clear to Carlos' mother that a decision such as this would be best made when the input of the father, as well as Carlos, is included in the final decision" (p. 63).

REFERENCES

American Psychological Association (APA). 1981. "Ethical Principles of Psychologists," *American Psychologist* **36** (6), 633.

Gert, B., and Culver, C. M. 1975. "The Justifications of Paternalism," *Ethics* **89,** 199.

Powell, C. J. 1984. "Ethical Principles and Issues of Competence in Counseling Adolescents," *The Counseling Psychologist* **12** (3), 57.

12

Consulting

Agencies look to consultants when they feel that their "in-house" professionals need help in dealing with an identified problem or concern. These groups then seek the assistance of a "technical expert" or "advisor" as a facilitator of change and a catalyst of problem resolution (Gallessick, 1982). A consultant is a professional within a particular field who has usually received specialized training in organizational development, group dynamics, problem-solving theory, and the like. The counselor/consultant is usually hired to advise on how to resolve a problem either at the agency level or at the client level. This means that such counselors will interact with at least two different publics: the agency that retained their services (in counsulting parlance, this body is called the client, but the helping professions call them counselees to avoid confusion with their own clients) and the individual or group within the agency for whom the specific services were procured (e.g., employees, clients, or both). The counselor/consultant does not work directly to solve problems. This means that the counselor/consultant serves simply as a catalyst to help the agency solve the problem. The counselor/consultant must resist being pushed into the role of problemsolver. It is all too easy for agencies to use consultants as scapegoats for unpopular decisions. Consultants are outsiders (Gallessick, 1982) to the groups with whom they interact, although in very large agencies it is not uncommon for them to come from another division or branch. The consulting relationship is very limited. It is for a brief period of time and for a very specific purpose defined in a contract between the consultant and the counselee.

Once the consultant's report has been issued, the job is finished (unless the consultee wishes to extend the contract or offer a new contract). It is the consultee's right to accept or reject the report's recommendations. "The consultee retains responsibility and authority" (Gallessick, 1982, p. 12) for follow-up action, including the implementation of any recommendations made by the consultant.

More counselors are engaging in consulting, either as a primary source of income or to supplement income from other sources. Counselors generally obtain consulting contracts either through solicitation or as an offshoot of other activities.

Counselors solicit consulting contracts by marketing their skills and availability. The most common forum used to promote their consulting skills is through a brochure. "Such brochures contain not only claims, testimonials, and aspects dealing with the desirability of the services and products offered, but also statements that solicit specific client/counselee populations. These same brochures often identify their professional staff as including counselors, social workers, nurses, administrators and educators" (Robinson & Gross, 1985, p. 451-52).

A counselor who promotes services via a brochure needs to ensure that the information contained in the direct mail piece is accurate and can be substantiated if challenged. It is the ethical responsibility of the counselor to make sure that the information provided does not create false expectations on the part of the client, and that it correctly reflects the counselor's expertise, qualifications, experience, education, and realistically describes the services provided.

The second method of obtaining clients is through invitation. This is the most common form of consulting entered into by counseling faculty. A client who wishes counseling services contacts the nearest university that offers counseling training in the hope of locating a member of the faculty who would be willing to serve as a consultant. This is so common among faculty that most colleges and universities have a rule (either written or assumed) that allows members of their faculties to devote up to twenty percent of their time in private consulting. Here again, counselors need to make sure that client expectations can be honestly fulfilled. Counselors need to understand what is expected within the consulting relationship, feel comfortable that they possess the skills necessary to deliver on the contract, and have the available time to ensure that any deadlines contained in the contract can be fully met.

One final forum through which counselors obtain consulting clients is as a byproduct of other professional activities: e.g., delivering papers or workshops at professional conferences, appearing on talk shows, or being quoted in the newspapers. When counselors promote themselves through such activities they should make sure that, where appropriate, clear disclaimers and qualifiers are included to protect against misleading or inaccurate information (Robinson & Gross, 1985).

There are a number of ethical issues to which counselors should be sensitive when entering the consulting environment. These include knowing who the client is, developing a consulting contract, and protecting the confidentiality of individuals and records.

When engaged in consulting, it is vital to know exactly who you are working for. When this question was addressed earlier, I discussed in some detail the ethical consequences of the answer for considerations of informed consent, working with minors, and so on. However, the question of client identity raises some unique ethical problems for the counselor/consultant. The following case study is illustrative:

> The executive director of a mid-sized firm referred a very ineffectual employee of the firm to Psychologist Q for an evaluation. The administrator and the psychologist agreed prior to the employee's first consultation that the psychologist would report back to the administrator as to whether the psychological evaluation indicated that it was feasible for the employee to continue in his position and, if so, whether remedial training would improve his performance. The employee saw Psychologist Q for several sessions of interviews and testing, assuming all that transpired during these sessions would be held confidential. Never doubting this, the employee did not raise questions about confidentiality and Psychologist Q did not explain her arrangement with the firm.
>
> Upon receipt of the psychologist's report, the executive director preemptorily fired the employee. Realizing for the first time what had occurred, the employee filed charges against Psychologist Q with the Ethics Committee. Psychologist Q responded to the Committee's inquiry that it was his understanding that the employer would brief the employee as to the nature of the evaluation and its possible implications for his continued employment with the firm. Assuming the company would do so, Psychologist Q said he saw no reason to raise the issue.
>
> Adjudication: The Ethics Committee found Psychologist Q in violation of Principle 6.b., having obviously failed to fulfill his responsibility

to clarify to the client the nature of the relationships between the three parties. Regardless of what the psychologist understood to be the employer's plans, it remained his ethical responsibility to be clear and explicit himself with the client. The Committee censured him. (APA, 1987, p. 85)

As this case illustrates, consulting contracts may involve multiple relationships each having obligations and expectations. It is important, therefore, for counselors to keep in mind that the client is the agency who hires their services. The first obligation is to the hiring agency and its official representative. "Consultants recognize the agency director, its chief executive officer, as the organization's official representative and final authority in making decisions. In all actions, consultants support this person's interpretation of agency interests (Gallessick, 1982, p. 397). In addition, the consulting contract may obligate the consultant to interact with one or more individuals, usually in the form of evaluation, assessment, training, development, or related function.

Not only must consultants clearly understand what each party expects from them, they are responsible for making sure that each party fully comprehends the nature of their joint relationship. In addition, consultants need to be sure that all parties have given their informed consent. Specifically, it is important that each party be informed of the process that will be undertaken, aware of potential risks and benefits, and cognizant of the right to make a free and uncoerced choice to participate, and the right to decline to participate at any time during the counseling process.

Lowman (1985) argues that while this is a sound principle, it may be naïve to believe that all employees are truly free to decline to participate. He cited the following example to prove his point. "An intervention team I was supervising once made the point that participation in an interview process of top managers was voluntary. A key manager declined to participate, feeling that the interviewers would be biased toward the family-member-owners who had brought them into the organization. No explanations or assurance could change this manager's mind. Although he was omitted from the interview process, he was negatively santioned by his superiors when they learned of his behavior" (p. 469).

The second major ethical concern unique to counselors who engage in consulting is the contract between the consultant and the employer. Robinson and Gross (1985) have done an excellent job of identifying these issues. Among them is the need for counselors to appreciate the fact that they enter the relationship from a position of power. Most of the time, the client will have little independent knowledge of the counselors' skills and ability to deliver the promised results. This point cannot be over-emphasized. The rule of *caveat emptor* (let the buyer beware) does not apply in professional relationships like that of consulting. It is well recognized (Robinson & Gross, 1985; Gallessick, 1982; Walter & Warwick, 1973) that the professional/client relationship is an unequal one with power vested for the most part in the professional. "Clients, as laypersons in the professional's speciality, lack sufficient information to judge whether a professional is competent and ethical. They must depend on the integrity of the professional for the choice of technology and its skilled applications. The gap between the knowledge of the professional and the layperson increases with specialization" (Gallessick, 1982, p. 391). Therefore, counselors are under an obligation to assess their skills and abilities honestly and to deliver the services called for by the contract. Glazer (1981) found that an ethical pitfall for many consultants is a failure to recognize their own "limitations of competence and to avoid making exaggerated claims" about their services (p. 14). A counselor "who creates, or knowingly allows the client to have, such exaggerated expectations is behaving unethically" (Walton & Warwick, 1973 p. 694).

An ethical problem also arises when in their enthusiasm to secure the contract counselors try to oversell the results they are capable of delivering. Glazer commented that "the role the consultant is willing to play can result in an ethical problem, particularly when he tries to apply a set package to too many different problems, agrees to a quick solution for a poorly defined problem, or begins intervention prior to assessing 'organizational readiness for given changes'" (Robinson & Gross, 1985, p. 454).

The ethical standards of the American Association for Counseling and Development stipulate that those of its members who engage in consulting insist that there "be [an] understanding and agreement between member and client for the problem definition, change of goals and predication of consequences of interventions selected" (AACD, 1988, p. 6).

This means that counselors should not enter into consulting contracts unless they believe that the relationships will be productive for the clients (Gallessick, 1982). In other words, the services consultants will provide must enhance the goals and objectives of the clients. If the consultants feel that their personal values conflict with the values of the clients, the counselors need to work with the clients in an attempt to resolve the differences but, if unsuccessful, the contract must be declined. Similarly, at the time of the contract negotiations, consultants must declare any conflict of interest and, if warranted, decline the contract.

Unfortunately, another ethical problem frequently arises in consulting relationships—viz., misunderstandings about the fee to be charged. Numerous consulting relationships turn acrimonious because counselors, who may be naïve in negotiating contracts, assume that certain costs will be reimbursed while the employer insists that if it isn't explicitly agreed to in writing, no payment will be made. Similarly, Glazer (1981) identified the "temptation to prolong the counseling engagement beyond what is needed/useful/productive, chiefly in order to continue billing" (quoted in Robinson & Gross, 1985, p. 455).

It is to everyone's mutual benefit that consultants require a prior written agreement that stipulates the amount of the fee (either an hourly rate or a flat fee) and all costs and expenses to be reimbursed (travel, materials, and the like). In addition, consultants should expect to provide clients with a complete accounting of time spent on the project and a list of all expenses with receipts attached (Robinson & Gross, 1985).

Unique problems of confidentiality arise for counselors who engage in consulting. Many times these problems are a result of the three-party nature of the counseling relationship: the counselor, the organization hiring the counselor (which is represented by its agents), and the individual with whom the counselor has been hired to interact (usually an employee of the organization). In many of these cases, the counselor is hired to evaluate the employee's performance, identify problem areas, and recommend solutions. In these situations counselors can find themselves in what Robinson and Gross (1985) call "the consultant's dilemma." This dilemma "is created by the tension between two powerful forces: (1) the employee whose rights the consultant respects and strives to protect and (2) the organization that wants to be informed about certain acts or intentions on the part of employees. How does one choose between the two?" (Robinson & Gross, 1985, p. 457). The answer is that the consultant needs to develop a clear understanding with all parties of what information will be shared with whom (Fanibanda, 1976). This understanding needs to be negotiated as a part of the consulting contract so that no party is confused as to what information will be shared with the employer and what information will be kept in confidence by the consultant. To do otherwise would be to act unethically.

A similar ethical problem arises with respect to the control of records kept during the consultation process. Again, there needs to be a clear understanding, agreed to in writing as part of the consulting contract, stating to whom the records belong and the nature and extent of said recording developed during the consulting process. In addition, there needs to be a prior understanding regarding what information is appropriate to be placed in the employee's personnel file. Many consultants have been shocked to discover that after having completed the consulting contract the information is used for purposes other than what the consultant understood to be its proper/appropriate use. Equally disturbing are reports that information provided by the consultant found its way into the employee's personnel file. The time to control the use of information and records is prior to its development. To put it another way, counselors are in the best position to safeguard confidentiality prior to the advent of the consulting relationship. In developing a strategy for the confidentiality of information and records, counselors are encouraged to consider carefully the following questions: "(1) What are the parameters of confidentiality? (2) How do I balance the organization's 'need to know' with the client/ employee's right to privacy? (3) What access do I and others have to employee files and what information should be placed in employee records? (4) Am I protecting the client/employee from coercion and manipulation and, if not, what are my responsibilities in this regard?" (Robinson & Gross, 1985, p. 458).

One more issue of confidentiality that needs to be touched upon is the question of the use of the information after completion of the consulting contract. Many times the counselor would like to use information gained from a specific consulting contract in a journal article or related publication. Others may wish to use some of the information as anecdotal material in a speech or as a demonstration of prior experience when soliciting new business.

It is unethical for counselors to use information in any of these forms without receiving prior written permission from all parties. When soliciting written permission counselors are obligated to make clear to each party the exact purpose for which the written permission is being sought and to restrict the use of that information only for the permitted purpose. To do anything different would be an unethical act.

Counselors who consider consulting are reminded to review the ethical standards of their profession to ensure that their actions conform to these standards. Some organizations, like the American Association for Counseling and Development, address ethical issues in consulting through specific sections of their codes while other organizations require that counselors adapt the general code to their special situations.

REFERENCES

American Association for Counseling and Development (AACD). 1988. *Ethical Standards of the AACD,* Alexandria, Va.: American Association for Counseling and Development.

American Psychological Association (APA). 1988. *Casebook on Ethical Principles of Psychologists,* Washington, D.C.: American Psychological Association, Inc.

Fanibanda, D. K. 1976. "Ethical Issues of Mental Health Consultants," *Professional Psychology* **7,** 547.

Gallessick, J. 1982. *The Profession and the Practice of Consultation,* San Francisco: Jossey-Bass.

Glazer, E. M. 1981. "Ethical Issues in Consultation Practice with Organizations," *Consultation* **1,** 12.

Lowman, R. L. 1985. "Ethical Practices of Psychological Consultations: Not an Impossible Dream," *The Consulting Pschologist* **13** (3), 466.

Robinson, S. E., and Gross, E. R. 1985. "Ethics in Consultations: The Canterville Ghost," *The Counseling Psychologist* **13,** 444.

Walton, R. E., and Warwick, D. P. 1973. "The Ethics of Organization," *Journal of Applied Behavioral Sciences* **9** (6), 681.

13

Conclusion

As we have seen, ethical issues in counseling comprise a unique study. This book, however, does not provide an easy answer to all ethical dilemmas. Its purpose, rather, is to sensitize the reader to the ethical issues faced by counselors. In the process, I have sought to raise "ethical consciousness." This has been done by employing the following method:

First, examples were provided of situations that you, the reader, may confront in your interactions with your clients. These examples are not designed to offer advice regarding how you ought to act, but rather to sensitize you to an awareness of how the ethical component of a problematic situation arises within counselor-client relationships.

Second, this book has sought to help counselors look at their own value system and, in a sense, provide a looking glass in which each individual can see reflected there who and what he or she is as a counselor. I hope you will be led to ask: "Am I everything I want to be? Are the values I see reflected the values I desire?"

Third, I have striven to provide a model for ethical analysis, a set of guidelines or a formula to help counselors successfully analyze these situations so that the ethical problems presented by the situations can be clearly understood and effectively confronted.

Additionally, I have sought to motivate those in the counseling profession to be ethical by looking at ethical problems from a clinical perspective. It is hoped that these cases will enable professionals to determine the right thing to do, which, in turn, will affect how counselors behave when confronted by similar circumstances in an actual counseling situation. Ideally, once examples are provided of ethical conduct in various counseling situations, you the professional will be personally motivated to be more ethical in your own conduct as a counselor.

It is my wish that this book may serve to motivate members of the counseling profession to raise the ethical standards of the profession and to insist that colleagues' behavior not only conform to the minimum standards of the profession, but that counselors serve as examples, in their public and private lives, of the best moral behavior.

Appendix

I have chosen to include in this Appendix only those codes of ethics which are most often cited in the text. Readers may wish to peruse these codes at their leisure in order to appreciate the context in which various cited sections appear. I have also included a list of the codes of ethics for the other major counseling organizations and the sources where these codes can be found.

Ethical Standards of the American Association of Counseling and Development

PREAMBLE

The Association is an educational, scientific, and professional organization whose members are dedicated to the enhancement of the worth, dignity, potential, and uniqueness of each individual and thus to the service of society.

The Association recognizes that the role definitions and work settings of its members include a wide variety of academic disciplines, levels of academic preparation, and agency services. This diversity reflects the breadth of the Association's interest and influence. It also poses challenging complexities in efforts to set standards for the performance of members, desired requisite preparation or practice, and supporting social, legal, and ethical controls.

The specification of ethical standards enables the Association to clarify

---

to present and future members and to those served by members the nature of ethical responsibilities held in common by its members.

The existence of such standards serves to stimulate greater concern by members for their own professional functioning and for the conduct of fellow professionals such as counselors, guidance and student personnel workers, and others in the helping professions. As the ethical code of the Association, this document establishes principles that define the ethical behavior of Association members. Additional ethical guidelines developed by the Association's Divisions for their specialty areas may further define a member's ethical behavior.

SECTION A: GENERAL

1. The member influences the development of the profession by continuous efforts to improve professional practices, teaching, services, and research. Professional growth is continuous throughout the member's career and is exemplified by the development of a philosophy that explains why and how a member functions in the helping relationship. Members must gather data on their effectiveness and be guided by the findings. Members recognize the need for continuing education to ensure competent service.

2. The member has a responsibility both to the individual who is served and to the institution within which the service is performed to maintain high standards of professional conduct. The member strives to maintain the highest levels of professional services offered to the individuals to be served. The member also strives to assist the agency, organization, or institution in providing the highest caliber of professional services. The acceptance of employment in an institution implies that the member is in agreement with the general policies and principles of the institution. Therefore the professional activities of the member are also in accord with the objectives of the institution. If, despite concerted efforts, the member cannot reach agreement with the employer as to acceptable standards of conduct that allow for changes in institutional policy conducive to the positive growth and development of clients, then terminating the affiliation should be seriously considered.

3. Ethical behavior among professional associates, both members and nonmembers, must be expected at all times. When information is possessed that raises doubt as to the ethical behavior of professional colleagues, whether Association members or not, the member must take action to attempt to rectify such a condition. Such action shall use the institu-

tion's channels first and then use procedures established by the Association.

4. The member neither claims nor implies professional qualifications exceeding those possessed and is responsible for correcting any misrepresentations of these qualifications by others.

5. In establishing fees for professional counseling services, members must consider the financial status of clients and locality. In the event that the established fee structure is inappropriate for a client, assistance must be provided in finding comparable services of acceptable cost.

6. When members provide information to the public or to subordinates, peers, or supervisors, they have a responsibility to ensure that the content is general, unidentified client information that is accurate, unbiased, and consists of objective, factual data.

7. Members recognize their boundaries of competence and provide only those services and use only those techniques for which they are qualified by training or experience. Members should only accept those positions for which they are professionally qualified.

8. In the counseling relationship, the counselor is aware of the intimacy of the relationship and maintains respect for the client and avoids engaging in activities that seek to meet the counselor's personal needs at the expense of that client.

9. Members do not condone or engage in sexual harassment which is defined as deliberate or repeated comments, gestures, or physical contacts of a sexual nature.

10. The member avoids bringing personal issues into the counseling relationship, especially if the potential for harm is present. Through awareness of the negative impact of both racial and sexual stereotyping and discrimination, the counselor guards the individual rights and personal dignity of the client in the counseling relationship.

11. Products or services provided by the member by means of classroom instruction, public lectures, demonstrations, written articles, radio or television programs, or other types of media must meet the criteria cited in these standards.

SECTION B: COUNSELING RELATIONSHIP

This section refers to practices and procedures of individual and/or group counseling relationships.

The member must recognize the need for client freedom of choice.

Under those circumstances where this is not possible, the member must apprise clients of restrictions that may limit their freedom of choice.

1. The member's primary obligation is to respect the integrity and promote the welfare of the client(s), whether the client(s) is (are) assisted individually or in a group relationship. In a group setting, the member is also responsible for taking reasonable precautions to protect individuals from physical and/or psychological trauma resulting from interaction within the group.

2. Members make provisions for maintaining confidentiality in the storage and disposal of records and follow an established record retention and disposition policy. The counseling relationship and information resulting therefrom must be kept confidential, consistent with the obligations of the member as a professional person. In a group counseling setting, the counselor must set a norm of confidentiality regarding all group participants' disclosures.

3. If an individual is already in a counseling relationship with another professional person, the member does not enter into a counseling relationship without first contacting and receiving the approval of that other professional. If the member discovers that the client is in another counseling relationship after the counseling relationship begins, the member must gain the consent of the other professional or terminate the relationship, unless the client elects to terminate the other relationship.

4. When the client's condition indicates that there is clear and imminent danger to the client or others, the member must take reasonable personal action or inform responsible authorities. Consultation with other professionals must be used where possible. The assumption of responsibility for the client's(s') behavior must be taken only after careful deliberation. The client must be involved in the resumption of responsibility as quickly as possible.

5. Records of the counseling relationship, including interview notes, test data, correspondence, tape recordings, and other documents, are to be considered professional information for use in counseling, and they should not be considered a part of the records of the institution or agency in which the counselor is employed unless specified by state statute or regulation. Revelation to others of counseling material must occur only upon the expressed consent of the client.

6. In view of the extensive data storage and processing capacities of the computer, the member must ensure that data maintained on a computer is: (a) limited to information that is appropriate and necessary for the services being provided; (b) destroyed after it is determined that

the information is no longer of any value in providing services; and (c) restricted in terms of access to appropriate staff members involved in the provision of services by using the best computer security methods available.

7. Use of data derived from a counseling relationship for purposes of counselor training or research shall be confined to content that can be disguised to ensure full protection of the identity of the subject client.

8. The member must inform the client of the purposes, goals, techniques, rules of procedure, and limitations that may affect the relationship at or before the time that the counseling relationship is entered. When working with minors or persons who are unable to give consent, the member protects these clients' best interests.

9. In view of common misconceptions related to the perceived inherent validity of computer-generated data and narrative reports, the member must ensure that the client is provided with information as part of the counseling relationship that adequately explains the limitations of computer technology.

10. The member must screen prospective group participants, especially when the emphasis is on self-understanding and growth through self-disclosure. The member must maintain an awareness of the group participants' compatibility throughout the life of the group.

11. The member may choose to consult with any other professionally competent person about a client. In choosing a consultant, the member must avoid placing the consultant in a conflict-of-interest situation that would preclude the consultant's being a proper party to the member's efforts to help the client.

12. If the member determines an inability to be of professional assistance to the client, the member must either avoid initiating the counseling relationship or immediately terminate that relationship. In either event, the member must suggest appropriate alternatives. (The member must be knowledgeable about referral resources so that a satisfactory referral can be initiated.) In the event the client declines the suggested referral, the member is not obligated to continue the relationship.

13. When the member has other relationships, particularly of an administrative, supervisory and/or evaluative nature with an individual seeking counseling services, the member must not serve as the counselor but should refer the individual to another professional. Only in instances where such an alternative is unavailable and where the individual's situation warrants counseling intervention should the member enter into and/or maintain a counseling relationship. Dual relationships with clients that might impair the member's objectivity and professional judgment (e.g., as with close

friends or relatives) must be avoided and/or the counseling relationship terminated through referral to another competent professional.

14. The member will avoid any type of sexual intimacies with clients. Sexual relationships with clients are unethical.

15. All experimental methods of treatment must be clearly indicated to prospective recipients, and safety precautions are to be adhered to by the member.

16. When computer applications are used as a component of counseling services, the member must ensure that: (a) the client is intellectually, emotionally, and physically capable of using the computer application; (b) the computer application is appropriate for the needs of the client; (c) the client understands the purpose and operation of the computer application; and (d) a follow-up of client use of a computer application is provided to both correct possible problems (misconceptions or inappropriate use) and assess subsequent needs.

17. When the member is engaged in short-term group treatment/ training programs (e.g., marathons and other encounter-type or growth groups), the member ensures that there is professional assistance available during the following the group experience.

18. Should the member be engaged in a work setting that calls for any variation from the above statements, the member is obligated to consult with other professionals whenever possible to consider justifiable alternatives.

19. The member must ensure that members of various ethnic, racial, religious, disability, and socioeconomic groups have equal access to computer applications used to support counseling services and that the content of available computer applications does not discriminate against the groups described above.

20. When computer applications are developed by the member for use by the general public as self-help/stand-alone computer software, the member must ensure that: (a) self-help computer applications are designed from the beginning to function in a stand-along manner, as opposed to modifying software that was originally designed to require support from a counselor; (b) self-help computer applications will include within the program statements regarding intended user outcomes, suggestions for using the software, a description of the conditions under which self-help computer applications might not be appropriate, and a description of when and how counseling services might be beneficial; and (c) the manual for such applications will include the qualifications of the developer, the development process, validation data, and operating procedures.

SECTION C: MEASUREMENT & EVALUATION

The primary purpose of educational and psychological testing is to provide descriptive measures that are objective and interpretable in either comparative or absolute terms. The member must recognize the need to interpret the statements that follow as applying to the whole range of appraisal techniques including test and nontest data. Test results constitute only one of a variety of pertinent sources of information for personnel, guidance, and counseling decisions.

1. The member must provide specific orientation or information to the examinee(s) prior to and following the test administration so that the results of testing may be placed in proper perspective with other relevant factors. In so doing, the member must recognize the effects of socioeconomic, ethnic, and cultural factors on test scores. It is the member's professional responsibility to use additional unvalidated information carefully in modfying interpretation of the test results.

2. In selecting tests for use in a given situation or with a particular client, the member must consider carefully the specific validity, reliability, and appropriateness of the test(s). General validity, reliability, and related issues may be questioned legally as well as ethically when tests are used for vocational and educational selection, placement, or counseling.

3. When making any statements to the public about tests and testing, the member must give accurate information and avoid false claims or misconceptions. Special efforts are often required to avoid unwarranted connotations of such terms as IQ and grade equivalent scores.

4. Different tests demand different levels of competence for administration, scoring, and interpretation. Members must recognize the limits of their competence and perform only those functions for which they are prepared. In particular, members using computer-based test interpretations must be trained in the construct being measured and the specific instrument being used prior to using this type of computer application.

5. In situations where a computer is used for test administration and scoring, the member is responsible for ensuring that administration and scoring programs function properly to provide clients with accurate test results.

6. Tests must be administered under the same conditions that were established in their standardization. When tests are not administered under standard conditions or when unusual behavior or irregularities occur during the testing session, those conditions must be noted and the results designated as invalid or of questionable validity. Unsupervised or inade-

quately supervised test-taking, such as the use of tests through the mails, is considered unethical. On the other hand, the use of instruments that are so designed or standardized to be self-administered and self-scored, such as interest inventories, is to be encouraged.

7. The meaningfulness of test results used in personnel, guidance, and counseling functions generally depends on the examinee's unfamiliarity with the specific items on the test. Any prior coaching or dissemination of the test materials can invalidate test results. Therefore, test security is one of the professional obligations of the member. Conditions that produce most favorable test results must be made known to the examinee.

8. The purpose of testing and the explicit use of the results must be made known to the examinee prior to testing. The counselor must ensure that instrument limitations are not exceeded and that periodic review and/or retesting are made to prevent client stereotyping.

9. The examinee's welfare and explicit prior understanding must be the criteria for determining the recipients of the test results. The member must see that specific interpretation accompanies any release of individual or group test data. The interpretation of test data must be related to the examinee's particular concerns.

10. Members responsible for making decisions based on test results have an understanding of educational and psychological measurement, validation criteria, and test research.

11. The member must be cautious when interpreting the results of research instruments possessing insufficient technical data. The specific purposes for the use of such instruments must be stated explicitly to examinees.

12. The member must proceed with caution when attempting to evaluate and interpret the performance of minority group members or other persons who are not represented in the norm group on which the instrument was standardized.

13. When computer-based test interpretations are developed by the member to support the assessment process, the member must ensure that the validity of such interpretations is established prior to the commercial distribution of such a computer application.

14. The member recognizes that test results may become obsolete. The member will avoid and prevent the misuse of obsolete test results.

15. The member must guard against the appropriation, reproduction, or modifications of published tests or parts thereof without acknowledgment and permission from the previous publisher.

16. Regarding the preparation, publication, and distribution of tests, reference should be made to:

a. "Standards for Educational and Psychological Testing," revised edition, 1985, published by the American Psychological Association on behalf of itself, the American Educational Research Association and the National Council of Measurement in Education.
b. "The Responsible Use of Tests: A Position Paper of AMEG, APGA, and NCME." *Measurement and Evaluation in Guidance,* 1972, 5, 385-88.
c. "Responsibilities of Users of Standardized Tests," APGA, *Guidepost,* October 5, 1978, pp. 5-8.

SECTION D: RESEARCH AND PUBLICATION

1. Guidelines on research with human subjects shall be adhered to, such as:
   a. *Ethical Principles in the Conduct of Research with Human Participants,* Washington, D.C.: American Psychological Association, Inc., 1982.
   b. Code of Federal Regulation, Title 45, Subtitle A, Part 46, as currently issued.
   c. *Ethical Principles of Psychologists,* American Psychological Association, Principle #9: Research with Human Participants.
   d. Family Educational Rights and Privacy Act (the Buckley Amendment).
   e. Current federal regulations and various state rights privacy acts.
2. In planning any research activity dealing with human subjects, the member must be aware of and responsive to all pertinent ethical principles and ensure that the research problem, design, and execution are in full compliance with them.
3. Responsibility for ethical research practice lies with the principal researcher, while others involved in the research activities share ethical obligation and full responsibility for their own actions.
4. In research with human subjects, researchers are responsible for the subjects' welfare throughout the experiment, and they must take all reasonable precautions to avoid causing injurious psychological, physical, or social effects on their subjects.
5. All research subjects must be informed of the purpose of the study except when withholding information or providing misinformation to them is essential to the investigation. In such research the member must be responsible for corrective action as soon as possible following completion of the research.

6. Participation in research must be voluntary. Involuntary participation is appropriate only when it can be demonstrated that participation will have no harmful effects on subjects and is essential to the investigation.

7. When reporting research results, explicit mention must be made of all variables and conditions known to the investigator that might affect the outcome of the investigation or the interpretation of the data.

8. The member must be responsible for conducting and reporting investigations in a manner that minimizes the possibility that results will be misleading.

9. The member has an obligation to make available sufficient original research data to qualified others who may wish to replicate the study.

10. When supplying data, aiding in the research of another person, reporting research results, or in making original data available, due care must be taken to disguise the identity of the subjects in the absence of specific authorization from such subjects to do otherwise.

11. When conducting and reporting research, the member must be familiar with and give recognition to previous work on the topic, as well as to observe all copyright laws and follow the principles of giving full credit to all to whom credit is due.

12. The member must give due credit through joint authorship, acknowledgment, footnote statements or other appropriate means to those who have contributed significantly to the research and/or publication, in accordance with such contributions.

13. The member must communicate to other members the results of any research judged to be of professional or scientific value. Results reflecting unfavorably on institutions, programs, services, or vested interests must not be withheld for such reasons.

14. If members agree to cooperate with another individual in research and/or publication, they incur an obligation to cooperate as promised in terms of punctuality of performance and with full regard to the completeness and accuracy of the information required.

15. Ethical practice requires that authors not submit the same manuscript or one essentially similar in content for simultaneous publication consideration by two or more journals. In addition, manuscripts published in whole or in substantial part in another journal or published work should not be submitted for publication without acknowledgment and permission from the previous publication.

SECTION E: CONSULTING

Consultation refers to a voluntary relationship between a professional helper and help-needing individual, group, or social unit in which the consultant is providing help to the client(s) in defining and solving a work-related problem or potential problem with a client or client system.

1. The member acting as consultant must have a high degree of self-awareness of his/her own values, knowledge, skills, limitations, and needs in entering a helping relationship that involves human and/or organizational change and that the focus of the relationship be on the issues to be resolved and not on the person(s) presenting the problem.

2. There must be understanding and agreement between member and client for the problem definition, change of goals, and prediction of consequences of interventions selected.

3. The member must be reasonably certain that she/he or the organization represented has the necessary competencies and resources for giving the kind of help that is needed now or may be needed later and that appropriate referral resources are available to the consultant.

4. The consulting relationship must be one in which client adaptability and growth toward self-direction are encouraged and cultivated. The member must maintain this role consistently and not become a decision maker for the client or create a future dependency on the consultant.

5. When announcing consultant availability for services, the member conscientiously adheres to the Association's Ethical Standards.

6. The member must refuse a private fee or other remuneration for consultation with persons who are entitled to these services through the member's employing institution or agency. The policies of a particular agency may make explicit provisions for private practice with agency clients by members of its staff. In such instances, the clients must be apprised of other options open to them should they seek private counseling services.

SECTION F: PRIVATE PRACTICE

1. The member should assist the profession by facilitating the availability of counseling services in private as well as public settings.

2. In advertising services as a private practitioner, the member must advertise the services in a manner that accurately informs the public of professional services, expertise, and techniques of counseling available. A member who assumes an executive leadership role in the organzation shall

not permit his/her name to be used in professional notices during periods when he/she is not actively engaged in the private practice of counseling.

3. The member may list the following: highest relevant degree, type and level of certification, and/or license, address, telephone number, office hours, type and/or description of services, and other relevant information. Such information must not contain false, inaccurate, misleading, partial, out-of-context, or deceptive material or statements.

4. Members do not present their affiliation with any organization in such a way that would imply inaccurate sponsorship or certification by that organization.

5. Members may join in partnership/corporation with other members and/or other professionals provided that each member of the partnership or corporation makes clear the separate specialties by name in compliance with the regulations of the locality.

6. A member has an obligation to withdraw from a counseling relationship of it is believed that employment will result in violation of the Ethical Standards. If the mental or physical condition of the member renders it difficult to carry out an effective professional relationship or if the member is discharged by the client because the counseling relationship is no longer productive for the client, then the member is obligated to terminate the counseling relationship.

7. A member must adhere to the regulations for private practice of the locality where the services are offered.

8. It is unethical to use one's institutional affiliation to recruit clients for one's private practice.

SECTION G: PERSONNEL ADMINISTRATION

It is recognized that most members are employed in public or quasi-public institutions. The functioning of a member within an institution must contribute to the goals of the institution and vice versa if either is to accomplish their respective goals or objectives. It is therefore essential that the member and the institution function in ways to: (a) make the institutional goals specific and public; (b) make the member's contribution to institutional goals specific; and (c) foster mutual accountability for goal achievement.

To accomplish these objectives, it is recognized that the member and the employer must share responsibilities in the formulation and implementation of personnel policies.

1. Members must define and describe the parameters and levels of their professional competency.

2. Members must establish interpersonal relations and working agreements with supervisors and subordinates regarding counseling or clinical relationships, confidentiality, distinction between public and private material, maintenance and dissemination of recorded information, work load, and accountability. Working agreements in each instance must be specified and made known to those concerned.

3. Members must alert their employers to conditions that may be potentially disruptive or damaging.

4. Members must inform employers of conditions that may limit their effectiveness.

5. Members must submit regularly to professional review and evaluation.

6. Members must be responsible for in-service development of self and/or staff.

7. Members must inform their staff of goals and programs.

8. Members must provide personnel practices that guarantee and enhance the rights and welfare of each recipient of their service.

9. Members must select competent persons and assign responsibilities compatible with their skills and experiences.

10. The member, at the onset of a counseling relationship, will inform the client of the member's intended use of supervisors regarding the disclosure of information concerning this case. The member will clearly inform the client of the limits of confidentiality in the relationship.

11. Members, as either employers or employees, do not engage in or condone practices that are inhumane, illegal, or unjustifiable (such as considerations based on sex, handicap, age, race) in hiring, promotion, or training.

SECTION H: PREPARATION STANDARDS

Members who are responsible for training others must be guided by the preparation standards of the Association and relevant Divisions(s). The member who functions in the capacity of trainer assumes unique ethical responsibilities that frequently go beyond that of the member who does not function in a training capacity. These ethical responsibilities are outlined as follows:

1. Members must orient students to program expectations, basic skills development, and employment prospects before admission to the program.

2. Members in charge of learning experiences must establish programs that integrate academic study and supervised practice.

3. Members must establish a program directed toward developing students' skills, knowledge, and self-understanding, stated whenever possible in competency or performance terms.

4. Members must identify the levels of competencies of their students in compliance with relevant Division standards. These competencies must accommodate the paraprofessional as well as the professional.

5. Members, through continual student evaluation and appraisal, must be aware of the personal limitations of the learner that might impede future performance. The instructor must not only assist the learner in securing remedial assistance but also screen from the program those individuals who are unable to provide competent services.

6. Members must provide a program that includes training in research commensurate with levels of role functioning. Paraprofessional and technician-level personnel must be trained as consumers of research. In addition, personnel must learn how to evaluate their own and their program's effectiveness. Graduate training, especially at the doctoral level, would include preparation for original research by the member.

7. Members must make students aware of the ethical responsibilities and standards of the profession.

8. Preparatory programs must encourage students to value the ideals of service to individuals and to society. In this regard, direct financial remuneration or lack thereof must not be allowed to overshadow professional and humanitarian needs.

9. Members responsible for educational programs must be skilled as teachers and practitioners.

10. Members must present thoroughly varied theoretical positions so that students may make comparisons and have the opportunity to select a position.

11. Members must develop clear policies within their educational institutions regarding field placement and the roles of the student and the instructor in such placement.

12. Members must ensure that forms of learning focusing on self-understanding or growth are voluntary or, if required as part of the education program, are made known to prospective students prior to entering the program. When the educational program offers a growth experience with an emphasis on self-disclosure or other relatively intimate or personal involvement, the member must have no administrative, supervisory, or evaluating authority regarding the participant.

13. The member will at all times provide students with clear and equally acceptable alternatives for self-understanding or growth experiences. The member will assure students that they have a right to accept these alternatives without prejudice or penalty.

14. Members must conduct an educational program in keeping with the current relevant guidelines of the Association.

Ethical Principles of Psychologists

PREAMBLE

Psychologists respect the dignity and worth of the individual and strive for the preservation and protection of fundamental human rights. They are committed to increasing knowledge of human behavior and of people's understanding of themselves and others and to the utilization of such knowledge for the promotion of human welfare. While pursuing these

---

From *American Psychologist* 36, no. 6 (June 1981: 633–38). Copyright © 1981 by the American Psychological Association. Reprinted by permission.

This version of the Ethical Principles of Psychologists (formerly entitled Ethical Standards of Psychologists) was adopted by the American Psychological Association's Council of Representatives on January 24, 1981. The revised Ethical Principles contain both substantive and grammatical changes in each of the nine ethical principles constituting the Ethical Standards of Psychologists previously adopted by the Council of Representatives in 1979, plus a new tenth principle entitled Care and Use of Animals. Inquiries concerning the Ethical Principles of Psychologists should be addressed to the Administrative Officer for Ethics, American Psychological Association, 1200 Seventeenth Street, N.W., Washington D.C. 20036.

These revised Ethical Principles apply to psychologists, to students of psychology, and to others who do work of a psychological nature under the supervision of a psychologist. They are also intended for the guidance of nonmembers of the Association who are engaged in psychological research or practice.

Any complaints of unethical conduct filed after January 24, 1981, shall be governed by this 1981 revision. However, conduct (a) complained about after January 24, 1981, but which occurred prior to that date, and (b) not considered unethical under prior versions of the principles but considered unethical under the 1981 revision, shall not be deemed a violation of ethical principles. Any complaints pending as of January 24, 1981, shall be governed either by the 1979 or by the 1981 version of the Ethical Principles, at the sound discretion of the Committee on Scientific and Professional Ethics and Conduct.

objectives, they make every effort to protect the welfare of those who seek their services and of the research participants that may be the object of study. They use their skills only for purposes consistent with these values and do not knowingly permit their misuse by others. While demanding for themselves freedom of inquiry and communication, psychologists accept the responsibility this freedom requires: competence, objectivity in the application of skills, and concern for the best interests of clients, colleagues, students, research participants, and society. In the pursuit of these ideals, psychologists subscribe to principles in the following areas: 1. Responsibility, 2. Competence, 3. Moral and Legal Standards, 4. Public Statements, 5. Confidentiality, 6. Welfare of the Consumer, 7. Professional Relationships, 8. Assessment Techniques, 9. Research With Human Participants, and 10. Care and Use of Animals.

Acceptance of membership in the American Psychological Association commits the member to adherence to these princples.

Psychologists cooperate with duly constituted committees of the American Psychological Association, in particular, the Committee on Scientific and Professional Ethics and Conduct, by responding to inquiries promptly and completely. Members also respond promptly and completely to inquiries from duly constituted state association ethics committees and professional standards review committees.

PRINCIPLE 1: RESPONSIBILITY

In providing services, psychologists maintain the highest standards of their profession. They accept responsibility for the consequences of their acts and make every effort to ensure that their services are used appropriately.

a. As scientists, psychologists accept responsibility for the selection of their research topics and the methods used in investigation, analysis, and reporting. They plan their research in ways to minimize the possibility that their findings will be misleading. They provide thorough discussion of the limitations of their data, especially where their work touches on social policy or might be misconstrued to the detriment of persons in specific age, sex, ethnic, socioeconomic, or other social groups. In publishing reports of their work, they never suppress disconfirming data, and they acknowledge the existence of alternative hypotheses and explanations of their findings. Psychologists take credit only for work they have actually done.

b. Psychologists clarify in advance with all appropriate persons and agencies the expectations for sharing and utilizing research data. They avoid relationships that may limit their objectivity or create a conflict of interest. Interference with the milieu in which data are collected is kept to a minimum.

c. Psychologists have the responsibility to attempt to prevent distortion, misuse, or suppression of psychological findings by the institution or agency of which they are employees.

d. As members of governmental or other organizational bodies, psychologists remain accountable as individuals to the highest standards of their profession.

e. As teachers, psychologists recognize their primary obligation to help others acquire knowledge and skill. They maintain high standards of scholarship by presenting psychological information objectively, fully, and accurately.

f. As practitioners, psychologists know that they bear a heavy social responsibility because their recommendations and professional actions may alter the lives of others. They are alert to personal, social, organizational, financial, or political situations and pressures that might lead to misuse of their influence.

PRINCIPLE 2: COMPETENCE

The maintenance of high standards of competence is a responsibility shared by all psychologists in the interest of the public and the profession as a whole. Psychologists recognize the boundaries of their competence and the limitations of their techniques. They only provide services and only use techniques for which they are qualified by training and experience. In those areas in which recognized standards do not yet exist, psychologists take whatever precautions are necessary to protect the welfare of their clients. They maintain knowledge of current scientific and professional information related to the services they render.

a. Psychologists accurately represent their competence, education, training, and experience. They claim as evidence of educational qualifications only those degrees obtained from institutions acceptable under the Bylaws and Rules of Council of the American Psychological Association.

b. As teachers, psychologists perform their duties on the basis of careful preparation so that their instruction is accurate, current, and scholarly.

c. Psychologists recognize the need for continuing education and are open to new procedures and changes in expectations and values over time.

d. Psychologists recognize differences among people, such as those that may be associated with age, sex, socioeconomic, and ethnic backgrounds. When necessary, they obtain training, experience, or counsel to assure competent service or research relating to such persons.

e. Psychologists responsible for decisions involving individuals or policies based on test results have an understanding of psychological or educational measurement, validation problems, and test research.

f. Psychologists recognize that personal problems and conflicts may interfere with professional effectiveness. Accordingly, they refrain from undertaking any activity in which their personal problems are likely to lead to inadequate performance or harm to a client, colleague, student, or research participant. If engaged in such activity when they become aware of their personal problems, they seek competent professional assistance to determine whether they should suspend, terminate, or limit the scope of their professional and/or scientific activities.

PRINCIPLE 3: MORAL AND LEGAL STANDARDS

Psychologists' moral and ethical standards of behavior are a personal matter to the same degree as they are for any other citizen, except as these may compromise the fulfillment of their professional responsibilities or reduce the public trust in psychology and psychologists. Regarding their own behavior, psychologists are sensitive to prevailing community standards and to the possible impact that conformity to or deviation from these standards may have upon the quality of their performance as psychologists. Psychologists are also aware of the possible impact of their public behavior upon the ability of colleagues to perform their professional duties.

a. As teachers, psychologists are aware of the fact that their personal values may affect the selection and presentation of instructional materials. When dealing with topics that may give offense, they recognize and respect the diverse attitudes that students may have toward such materials.

b. As employees or employers, psychologists do not engage in or condone practices that are inhumane or that result in illegal or unjustifiable actions. Such practices include, but are not limited to, those based on considerations of race, handicap, age, gender, sexual preference, religion, or national origin in hiring, promotion, or training.

c. In their professional roles, psychologists avoid any action that will violate or diminish the legal and civil rights of clients or of others who may be affected by their actions.

d. As practitioners and researchers, psychologists act in accord with Association standards and guidelines related to practice and to the conduct of research with human beings and animals. In the ordinary course of events, psychologists adhere to relevant governmental laws and institutional regulations. When federal, state, provincial, organizational, or institutional laws, regulations, or practices are in conflict with Association standards and guidelines, psychologists make known their commitment to Association standards and guidelines and, wherever possible, work toward a resolution of the conflict. Both practitioners and researchers are concerned with the development of such legal and quasi-legal regulations as best serve the public interest, and they work toward changing existing regulations that are not beneficial to the public interest.

PRINCIPLE 4: PUBLIC STATEMENTS

Public statements, announcements of services, advertising, and promotional activities of psychologists serve the purpose of helping the public make informed judgments and choices. Psychologists represent accurately and objectively their professional qualifications, affiliations, and functions, as well as those of the institutions or organizations with which they or the statements may be associated. In public statements providing psychological information or professional opinions or providing information about the availability of psychological products, publications, and services, psychologists base their statements on scientifically acceptable psychological findings and techniques with full recognition of the limits and uncertainties of such evidence.

a. When announcing or advertising professional services, psychologists may list the following information to describe the provider and services provided: name, highest relevant academic degree earned from a regionally accredited institution, date, type, and level of certification or licensure, diplomate status, APA membership status, address, telephone number, office hours, a brief listing of the type of psychological services offered, an appropriate presentation of fee information, foreign languages spoken, and policy with regard to third-party payments. Additional relevant or important consumer information may be included if not prohibited by other sections of these Ethical Principles.

b. In announcing or advertising the availability of psychological products, publications, or services, psychologists do not present their affiliation with any organization in a manner that falsely implies sponsorship or certification by that organization. In particular and for example, psychologists do not state APA membership or fellow status in a way to suggest that such status implies specialized professional competence or qualifications. Public statements include, but are not limited to, communication by means of periodical, book, list, directory, television, radio, or motion picture. They do not contain (i) a false, fraudulent, misleading, deceptive, or unfair statement; (ii) a misinterpretation of fact or a statement likely to mislead or deceive because in context it makes only a partial disclosure of relevant facts; (iii) a testimonial from a patient regarding the quality of a psychologist's services or products; (iv) a statement intended or likely to create false or unjustified expectations of favorable results; (v) a statement implying unusual, unique, or one-of-a-kind abilities; (vi) a statement intended or likely to appeal to a client's fears, anxieties, or emotions concerning the possible results of failure to obtain the offered services; (vii) a statement concerning the comparative desirability of offered services; (viii) a statement of direct solicitation of individual clients.

c. Psychologists do not compensate or give anything of value to a representative of the press, radio, television, or other communication medium in anticipation of or in return for professional publicity in a news item. A paid advertisement must be identified as such, unless it is apparent from the context that it is a paid advertisement. If communicated to the public by use of radio or television, an advertisement is prerecorded and approved for broadcast by the psychologist, and a recording of the actual transmission is retained by the psychologist.

d. Announcements or advertisements of "personal growth groups," clinics, and agencies give a clear statement of purpose and a clear description of the experiences to be provided. The education, training, and experience of the staff members are appropriately specified.

e. Psychologists associated with the development or promotion of psychological devices, books, or other products offered for commercial sale make reasonable efforts to ensure that announcements and advertisements are presented in a professional, scientifically acceptable, and factually informative manner.

f. Psychologists do not participate for personal gain in commercial announcements or advertisements recommending to the public the purchase or use of proprietary or single-source products or services when that participation is based solely upon their identification as psychologists.

g. Psychologists present the science of psychology and offer their services, products, and publications fairly and accurately, avoiding misrepresentation through sensationalism, exaggeration, or superficiality. Psychologists are guided by the primary obligation to aid the public in developing informed judgments, opinions, and choices.

h. As teachers, psychologists ensure that statements in catalogs and course outlines are accurate and not misleading, particularly in terms of subject matter to be covered, bases for evaluating progress, and the nature of course experiences. Announcements, brochures, or advertisements describing workshops, seminars, or other educational programs accurately describe the audience for which the program is intended as well as eligibility requirements, educational objectives, and nature of the materials to be covered. These announcements also accurately represent the education, training, and experience of the psychologists presenting the programs and any fees involved.

i. Public announcements or advertisements soliciting research participants in which clinical services or other professional services are offered as an inducement make clear the nature of the services as well as the costs and other obligations to be accepted by participants in the research.

j. A psychologist accepts the obligation to correct others who may represent the psychologist's professional qualifications, or associations with products or services, in a manner incompatible with these guidelines.

k. Individual diagnostic and therapeutic services are provided only in the context of a professional psychological relationship. When personal advice is given by means of public lectures or demonstrations, newspaper or magazine articles, radio or television programs, mail, or similar media, the psychologist utilizes the most current relevant data and exercises the highest level of professional judgment.

l. Products that are described or presented by means of public lectures or demonstrations, newspaper or magazine articles, radio or television programs, or similar media meet the same recognized standards as exist for products used in the context of a professional relationship.

PRINCIPLE 5: CONFIDENTIALITY

Psychologists have a primary obligation to respect the confidentiality of information obtained from persons in the course of their work as psychologists. They reveal such information to others only with the consent of the person or the person's legal representative, except in those unusual circumstances in which not to do so would result in clear danger to the person or to others. Where appropriate, psychologists inform their clients of the legal limits of confidentiality.

a. Information obtained in clinical or consulting relationships, or evaluative data concerning children, students, employees, and others, is discussed only for professional purposes and only with persons clearly concerned with the case. Written and oral reports present only data germane to the purposes of the evaluation, and every effort is made to avoid undue invasion of privacy.

b. Psychologists who present personal information obtained during the course of professional work in writings, lectures, or other public forums either obtain adequate prior consent to do so or adequately disguise all identifying information.

c. Psychologists make provisions for maintaining confidentiality in the storage and disposal of records.

d. When working with minors or other persons who are unable to give voluntary, informed consent, psychologists take special care to protect these persons' best interests.

PRINCIPLE 6: WELFARE OF THE CONSUMER

Psychologists respect the integrity and protect the welfare of the people and groups with whom they work. When conflicts of interest arise between clients and psychologists' employing institutions, psychologists clarify the nature and direction of their loyalties and responsibilities and keep all parties informed of their commitments. Psychologists fully inform consumers as to the purpose and nature of an evaluative, treatment, educational, or training procedure, and they freely acknowledge that clients, students, or participants in research have freedom of choice with regard to participation.

a. Psychologists are continually cognizant both of their own needs and of their potentially influential position vis-à-vis persons such as clients, students, and subordinates. They avoid exploiting the trust and dependency of such persons. Psychologists make every effort to avoid dual relationships that could impair their professional judgment or increase the risk of exploitation. Examples of such dual relationships include, but are not limited to, research with and treatment of employees, students, supervisees, close friends, or relatives. Sexual intimacies with clients are unethical.

b. When a psychologist agrees to provide services to a client at the request of a third party, the psychologist assumes the responsibility of clarifying the nature of the relationships to all parties concerned.

c. Where the demands of an organization require psychologists to violate these Ethical Principles, psychologists clarify the nature of the conflict between the demands and these principles. They inform all parties of psychologists' ethical responsibilities and take appropriate action.

d. Psychologists make advance financial arrangements that safeguard the best interests of and are clearly understood by their clients. They neither give nor receive any remuneration for referring clients for professional services. They contribute a portion of their services to work for which they receive little or no financial return.

e. Psychologists terminate a clinical or consulting relationship when it is reasonably clear that the consumer is not benefiting from it. They offer to help the consumer locate alternative sources of assistance.

PRINCIPLE 7: PROFESSIONAL RELATIONSHIPS

Psychologists act with due regard for the needs, special competencies, and obligations of their colleagues in psychology and other professions. They respect the prerogatives and obligations of the institutions or organizations with which these other colleagues are associated.

a. Psychologists understand the areas of competence of related professions. They make full use of all the professional, technical, and administrative resources that serve the best interests of consumers. The absence of formal relationships with other professional workers does not relieve psychologists of the responsibility of securing for their clients the best possible professional service, nor does it relieve them of the obligation to exercise foresight, diligence, and tact in obtaining the complementary or alternative assistance needed by clients.

b. Psychologists know and take into account the traditions and practices of other professional groups with whom they work and cooperate fully with such groups. If a person is receiving similar services from another professional, psychologists do not offer their own services directly to such a person. If a psychologist is contacted by a person who is already receiving similar services from another professional, the psychologist carefully considers that professional relationship and proceeds with caution and sensitivity to the therapeutic issues as well as the client's welfare. The psychologist discusses these issues with the client so as to minimize the risk of confusion and conflict.

c. Psychologists who employ or supervise other professionals or professionals in training accept the obligation to facilitate the further professional development of these individuals. They provide appropriate working conditions, timely evaluations, constructive consultation, and experience opportunities.

d. Psychologists do not exploit their professional relationships with clients, supervisees, students, employees, or research participants sexually or otherwise. Psychologists do not condone or engage in sexual harassment. Sexual harassment is defined as deliberate or repeated comments, gestures, or physical contacts of a sexual nature that are unwanted by the recipient.

e. In conducting research in institutions or organizations, psychologists secure appropriate authorization to conduct such research. They are aware of their obligations to future research workers and ensure that host institutions receive adequate information about the research and proper acknowlegment of their contributions.

f. Publication credit is assigned to those who have contributed to a publication in proportion to their professional contributions. Major contributions of a professional character made by several persons to a common project are recognized by joint authorship, with the individual who made the principal contribution listed first. Minor contributions of a professional character and extensive clerical or similar nonprofessional assistance may be acknowledged in footnotes or in an introductory statement. Acknowledgment through specific citations is made for unpublished as well as published material that has directly influenced the research or writing. Psychologists who compile and edit material of others for publication publish the material in the name of the originating group, if appropriate, with their own name appearing as chairperson or editor. All contributors are to be acknowledged and named.

g. When psychologists know of an ethical violation by another psychologist, and it seems appropriate, they informally attempt to resolve the issue by bringing the behavior to the attention of the psychologist. If the misconduct is of a minor nature and/or appears to be due to lack of sensitivity, knowledge, or experience, such an informal solution is usually appropriate. Such informal corrective efforts are made with sensitivity to any rights to confidentiality involved. If the violation does not seem amenable to an informal solution, or is of a more serious nature, psychologists bring it to the attention of the appropriate local, state, and/or national committee on professional ethics and conduct.

PRINCIPLE 8: ASSESSMENT TECHNIQUES

In the development, publication, and utilization of psychological assessment techniques, psychologists make every effort to promote the welfare and best interests of the client. They guard against the misuse of assessment results. They respect the client's right to know the results, the interpreta-

tions made, and the bases for their conclusions and recommendations. Psychologists make every effort to maintain the security of tests and other assessment techniques within limits of legal mandates. They strive to ensure the appropriate use of assessment techniques by others.

a. In using assessment techniques, psychologists respect the right of the clients to have full explanations of the nature and purpose of the techniques in language the clients can understand, unless an explicit exception to this right has been agreed upon in advance. When the explanations are to be provided by others, psychologists establish procedures for ensuring the adequacy of these explanations.

b. Psychologists responsible for the development and standardization of psychological tests and other assessment techniques utilize established scientific procedures and observe the relevant APA standards.

c. In reporting assessment results, psychologists indicate any reservations that exist regarding validity or reliability because of the circumstances of the assessment or the inappropriateness of the norms for the person tested. Psychologists strive to ensure that the results of assessments and their interpretations are not misused by others.

d. Psychologists recognize that assessment results may become obsolete. They make every effort to avoid and prevent the misuse of obsolete measures.

e. Psychologists offering scoring and interpretation services are able to produce appropriate evidence for the validity of the programs and procedures used in arriving at interpretations. The public offering of an automated interpretation service is considered a professional-to-professional consultation. Psychologists make every effort to avoid misuse of assessment reports.

f. Psychologists do not encourage or promote the use of psychological assessment techniques by inappropriately trained or otherwise unqualified persons through teaching, sponsorship, or supervision.

PRINCIPLE 9: RESEARCH WITH HUMAN PARTICIPANTS

The decision to undertake research rests upon a considered judgment by the individual psychologist about how best to contribute to psychological science and human welfare. Having made the decision to conduct research, the psychologist considers alternative directions in which research energies and resources might be invested. On the basis of this consideration, the psychologist carries out the investigation with respect and concern for the dignity and welfare of the people who participate and with cognizance of federal and state regulations and professional standards governing the conduct of research with human participants.

a. In planning a study, the investigator has the responsibility to make a careful evaluation of its ethical acceptability. To the extent that the weighing of scientific and human values suggests a compromise of any principle, the investigator incurs a correspondingly serious obligation to seek ethical advice and to observe stringent safeguards to protect the rights of human participants.

b. Considering whether a participant in a planned study will be a "subject at risk" or a "subject at minimal risk," according to recognized standards, is of primary ethical concern to the investigator.

c. The investigator always retains the responsibility for ensuring ethical practice in research. The investigator is also responsible for the ethical treatment of research participants by collaborators, assistants, students, and employees, all of whom, however, incur similar obligations.

d. Except in minimal-risk research, the investigator establishes a clear and fair agreement with research participants, prior to their participation, that clarifies the obligations and responsibilities of each. The investigator has the obligation to honor all promises and commitments included in that agreement. The investigator informs the participants of all aspects of the research that might reasonably be expected to influence willingness to participate and explains all other aspects of the research about which the participants inquire. Failure to make full disclosure prior to obtaining informed consent requires additional safeguards to protect the welfare and dignity of the research participants. Research with children or with participants who have impairments that would limit understanding and/or communication requires special safeguarding procedures.

e. Methodological requirements of a study may make the use of concealment or deception necessary. Before conducting such a study, the investigator has a special responsibility to (i) determine whether the use of such techniques is justified by the study's prospective scientific, educational, or applied value; (ii) determine whether alternative procedures are available that do not use concealment or deception; and (iii) ensure that the participants are provided with sufficient explanation as soon as possible.

f. The investigator respects the individual's freedom to decline to participate in or to withdraw from the research at any time. The obligation to protect this freedom requires careful thought and consideration when the investigator is in a position of authority or influence over the participant. Such positions of authority include, but are not limited to, situations in which research participation is required as part of employment or in which the participant is a student, client, or employee of the investigator.

g. The investigator protects the participant from physical and mental discomfort, harm, and danger that may arise from research procedures. If risks of such consequences exist, the investigator informs the participant of that fact. Research procedures likely to cause serious or lasting harm to a participant are not used unless the failure to use these procedures might expose the participant to risk of greater harm, or unless the research has great potential benefit and fully informed and voluntary consent is obtained from each participant. The participant should be informed of procedures for contacting the investigator within a reasonable time period following participation should stress, potential harm, or related questions or concerns arise.

h. After the data are collected, the investigator provides the participant with information about the nature of the study and attempts to remove any misconceptions that may have arisen. Where scientific or humane values justify delaying or withholding this information, the investigator incurs a special responsibility to monitor the research and to ensure that there are no damaging consequences for the participant.

i. Where research procedures result in undesirable consequences for the individual participant, the investigator has the responsibility to detect and remove or correct these consequences, including long-term effects.

j. Information obtained about a research participant during the course of an investigation is confidential unless otherwise agreed upon in advance. When the possibility exists that others may obtain access to such information, this possibility, together with the plans for protecting confidentiality, is explained to the participant as a part of the procedure for obtaining informed consent.

PRINCIPLE 10: CARE AND USE OF ANIMALS

An investigator of animal behavior strives to advance understanding of basic behavioral principles and/or to contribute to the improvement of human health and welfare. In seeking these ends, the investigator ensures the welfare of animals and treats them humanely. Laws and regulations notwithstanding, an animal's immediate protection depends upon the scientist's own conscience.

a. The acquisition, care, use, and disposal of all animals are in compliance with current federal, state or provincial, and local laws and regulations.

b. A psychologist trained in research methods and experienced in the care of laboratory animals closely supervises all procedures involving animals and is responsible for ensuring appropriate consideration of their comfort, health, and humane treatment.

c. Psychologists ensure that all individuals using animals under their supervision have received explicit instruction in experimental methods and in the care, maintenance, and handling of the species being used. Responsibilities and activities of individuals participating in a research project are consistent with their respective competencies.

d. Psychologists make every effort to minimize discomfort, illness, and pain of animals. A procedure subjecting animals to pain, stress, or privation is used only when an alternative procedure is unavailable and the goal is justified by its prospective scientific, educational, or applied value. Surgical procedures are performed under appropriate anesthesia; techniques to avoid infection and minimize pain are followed during and after surgery.

e. When it is appropriate that the animal's life be terminated, it is done rapidly and painlessly.

Bibliography of Ethical Codes

American Association for Marriage and Family Therapy. 1984. *Ethical Principles for Family Therapists* (pamphlet). Washington, D.C.: Author.

American Association for Marriage and Family Therapy. 1985. *Code of Ethical Principles for Marriage and Family Therapists*. Washington, D.C.: Author.

American Association for Sex Educators, Counselors, and Therapists. 1980. *Code of Ethics*. Washington, D.C.: Author.

American College Personnel Association. 1980. *Statement of Ethical and Professional Standards*. Alexandria, Va.: American Association for Counseling and Development.

American Group Psychotherapy Association. 1978. *Guidelines for the Training of Group Psychotherapists*. New York, N.Y.: Author.

American Mental Health Counselors Association. 1980. *Code of Ethics for Certified Clinical Mental Health Counselors*. Falls Church, Va.: Author.

American Psychiatric Association. 1986. *Principles of Medical Ethics, with Annotations Especially Applicable to Psychiatry*. Washington, D.C.: Author.

American Psychological Association. 1977. "Standards for Providers of Psychological Services," *American Psychologist* **32,** 495.

173

American Psychological Association. 1981a. "Specialty Guidelines for the Delivery of Services," *American Psychologist* **36** (6), 639.

American Psychological Association. Division of Counseling Psychology. 1979. "Principles Concerning the Counseling and Therapy of Women," *The Counseling Psychologist* **8** (1), 21.

American Psychological Association. 1985. "Rules of Procedure: Ethics Committee of the American Psychological Association," *American Psychologist* **40** (6), 685.

American School Counselor Association. 1984. *Ethical Standards for School Counselors.* Alexandria, Va.: Author.

Commission on Rehabilitation Counselor Certification. *Code of Ethics.* Arlington Heights, Ill.: Author.

National Association of Social Workers. 1979. *Code of Ethics.* Silver Spring, Md.: Author.